Being Torah

A First Book Of Torah Texts

Text by **Joel Lurie Grishaver** with **Jane Ellen Golub** • **Alan Brahm Rowe**
• Cover Photograph by **Hilda Cohen** • Text Photography by **Hilda
Cohen** • **Jane Ellen Golub** • and **Alan Brahm Rowe** • **Steven
Feinholz**

TORAH AURA PRODUCTIONS

For Shirley Barish, who stands as a paradigm of dedication and excellence in the world of Jewish Education.

Acknowledgements:

This work has evolved through the insight and support of a number of good friends. It was inspired by a number of congregational educators. Specifically, Paul Flexner, Melanie Berman, Joyce Seglin and Janice Alper were foundational to the decision to attempt this work and to the work's direction. Throughout the process, my two business partners, Jane Golub and Alan Rowe, tolerated and supported the creative process. My thanks go to Everett Fox, whose Shocken translation, **In the Beginning**, was inspirational for this rendition. Finally, we owe a significant debt to two friends who have helped us to shape and perfect this material, thereby helping to pragmatize our vision. Rabbi Joel Gordon consulted on the accuracy of the translation and the appropriateness of work material. Seymour Rossel served as editor, and helped to clarify and sharpen the manuscript. Without Seymour's careful pruning, this work would not have successfully emerged from it creative tangle. My thanks to all involved.

Joel Lurie Grishaver

12 Tammuz 5445

Library of Congress Cataloging-In-Publication Data

Grishaver, Joel Lurie.
   Being Torah.

   Summary: A collection of stories, commentaries, and exercises based on the Biblical books of Genesis and Exodus.
   1. Bible. O.T. Genesis—Juvenile literature. 2. Bible. O.T. Exodus—Juvenile literature. [1. Bible stories—O.T.] I. Golub, Jane Ellen. II. Cohen, Hilda, ill. III. Rowe, Alan Brahm. IV. Title.
BS1239.G75 1986   222'.11077   86-16096
ISBN 0-933873-00-X (pbk.)

© 1985 Torah Aura Productions   Revised edition, 1986
      4423 Fruitland Ave.   3RD Printing
      Los Angeles, California 90058

Manufactured in The United States of America

CONTENTS

FOR PARENTS AND TEACHERS

It is easy to imagine that many of the Torah's stories were first told around a campfire. The Torah is filled with exciting images that a listener needs to picture in his or her mind. We are taken on a stormy ride on a boat filled with animals, and then shown a peaceful rainbow. We look up a ladder ascending into the heavens and then wrestle a stranger in the dark. We are given a coat of many colors, thrown in pit, and then emerge to hear more dreams. The Torah has an oral impact. It haunts the listener with images, introduces him or her to significant role models, and evolves the first layer of a moral fabric. Like our ancestors, most children first encounter the oral dynamic of Torah, hearing its stories long before they study its texts. They are told or read stories which become the basis for crafts, drama, discussion, and other extensions of imagination.

The Torah, however, is more than a collection of bedtime stories. Its stories are precisely crafted texts that need careful closereading. Much of the Torah's depth comes from the way its stories are told. When we do look closely, we find stories written in specific patterns, with words being reused specific numbers of times, with significant insight being communicated through subtle word changes, and with word-symbols being evolved through a series of usages. We are taught to be "keepers," first of a garden, then of our brother, and finally of a covenant. We are made to feel like "strangers" in Canaan, "strangers" in Egypt, and then are taught to protect and help the "stranger in our midst." Moving through the mythic fabric of the Torah's tales is the concise evolution of a significant vocabulary of Jewish existence. The Jewish people's relationship with Torah is indeed rooted in an oral experience, but its foundation lies in the close reading of its text.

BEING TORAH has been designed to begin the development of this second relationship with Torah. It has been crafted so second to fourth grade students can apply their emerging reading skills to unlock their own discovered meanings in the Torah's texts. To facilitate this relationship, **BEING TORAH** has been constructed around special translations of the masoritic text. These have been designed to be true to the patterns, language, and style of the original, while limiting the vocabulary and syntactic complexity of the English. These translations have been prompted to reveal "theme-words," "word-echoes," and other elements of narrative artistry. In addition, the material has been edited to provide sequences of usable length and to allow for a nonsexist first encounter with this core source.

Accompanying these translations are three tools. After almost every chapter there is a set of Commentaries. Here, voiced as children's responses, is a set of model reactions to the text. These serve as discussion triggers. Next is a section called "A Close Look." This helps **students** to focus on the messages built out of the text's narrative, and to explore key biblical phrases. Finally, at the back of the book, are the answers which go beyond being a self-checking device toward setting the direction for additional discussion and learning. Used together, these tools make **BEING TORAH** the perfect book to introduce a child to Torah.

BEING TORAH

Around 300 years ago there was a famous rabbi named Dov. People used to call Dov **The Magid**. **Magid** means story teller. He was a very famous teacher, and students came from everywhere to study Torah with him. The students used to try to remember every single thing he taught. They thought if they could repeat every lesson and insight, they would really know Torah.

The **Magid** however, had one special lesson. He used to tell his students:

DON'T JUST SAY WORDS OF TORAH
BE TORAH

This book is all about **BEING TORAH**.

Sometimes you may find yourself walking down the street and singing a song you heard on the radio or that you just heard on your stereo. Often you don't even remember deciding to sing that song. It is just a part of you that came out on its own. Being Torah is like that, too.

The Torah contains lots of stories that are told in special ways. Both the stories and how they are told are important. This book can help you discover the power in the words which make up the Torah. Soon you may find yourself walking down the street and thinking of words like **God's image, brother's keeper,** or **remember the covenant**. Making these words part of you is really **BEING TORAH**.

Joel Lurie Grishaver

COMMENTARY

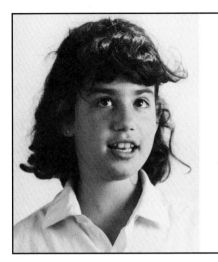

The Torah is something that every Jew studies. At my cousin's Bat Mitzvah they had my grandmother come up and hand the Torah to Uncle David, who handed it to my cousin Debby. Jews are always passing the Torah from one person to another. It is not just handing the scroll from one person to another. It is also passing all the wisdom and all of the tradition. Being Torah is learning all about the Torah and passing that on to other people.

Shelly

Bible stories aren't fairy tales. When you read the Torah, you don't find any dragons, witches, knights, or castles. The people in the Bible are heros because they are usually trying to become the best they can be by learning from God. Being Torah is joining Noah, Abraham, Sarah, and Moses in becoming the best possible you that you can be. Studying Torah is like having God as a teacher.

Josh

When I was really little, and before I could read on my own, one of my parents would sometimes read me a Bible story before I went to sleep. Other times they would tell me a story where I was part of the story and where I would help the hero in the end. Now I can read for myself and I even do it under the covers with my flashlight. I still like to pretend that I am part of the story. I guess Being Torah means seeing myself as part of the Torah.

Jennifer

CHAPTER 1 **BEGINNINGS** Genesis 1:1-2:3

בְּרֵאשִׁית בָּרָא אֱלֹהִים
אֵת הַשָּׁמַיִם
וְאֵת הָאָרֶץ

BEGINNINGS:
God **created** the heavens and the earth.
The earth was unformed.
Darkness was over the deep.
The breath of God was over the waters.

יוֹם אֶחָד

*God said: "Let there be light."
And there was light.
God said: "GOOD."

God called the light: "Day."
God called the darkness: "Night."

There was evening.
There was morning.
Day one.

יוֹם שֵׁנִי

*God said: "Let there be a space between the waters."
And God made the space.
God called the space: "Sky."

There was evening.
There was morning.
A second day.

יוֹם שְׁלִישִׁי

*God said: "Let dry land appear."
And it was so.
God called the dry land: "Earth."
God called the waters: "Sea."
God said: "GOOD."

*God said: "Let plants and green things grow."
And it was so.
God said: "GOOD."

There was evening.
There was morning.
A third day.

יוֹם רְבִיעִי

*God said: "Let there be lights in the sky.
They will be signs for the seasons,
for the days and for the years."
And it was so.
God made two great lights.
One light to shine during the day.
One light to shine at night.
And the stars, too,
God placed them in the sky, to give light on the earth
and to divide between light and darkness.
God said: "GOOD."

There was evening.
There was morning.
A fourth day.

יוֹם חֲמִישִׁי

*God said: "Let the waters swim with life.
And let the sky be filled with birds."
And God **created** the great sea-serpents,
and the crawling things which filled the waters,
and the birds, too.
God said: "GOOD."

God blessed them: "Be fruitful,
and become many,
and fill the waters and the sky."

There was evening.
There was morning.
A fifth day.

יוֹם הַשִּׁשִׁי

*God said: "Let there be wildlife on the earth."
God made the wildlife.
There were beasts and creeping things.
God said: "GOOD."

*God said: "Let Us make people in Our image.
Let them rule over the fish and the birds,
over the beasts and the creeping things."
God made people in God's image.
God **created** people—both man and woman.

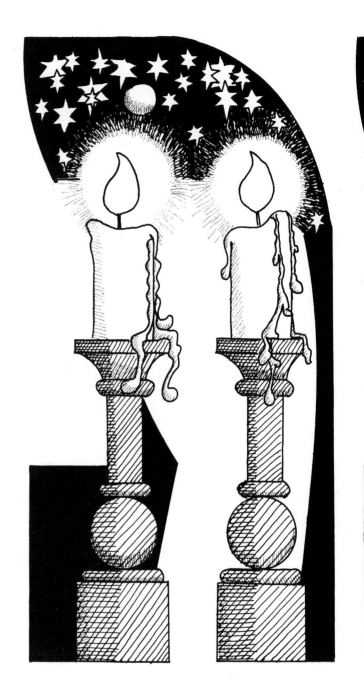

בְּצֶלֶם אֱלֹהִים בָּרָא אֹתוֹ

God blessed them:
*God said to them:
"Be fruitful,
and become many,
and fill the earth
and master it."

*God said: "I give you
all plants and all trees
for your food."

God saw everything
God had made.
God said:"Very GOOD."

There was evening.
There was morning.
The sixth day.

וַיְכֻלּוּ הַשָּׁמַיִם וְהָאָרֶץ
וְכָל־צְבָאָם

The heavens and the earth were finished.
God finished all the work on the seventh day.
On the seventh day God rested from all the work.

God blessed the seventh day and made it holy,
because on it God rested from all the work.
Everything had been **created**.

COMMENTARY

When I read this story, I imagine taking a walk with God. When we pass something God created, God says: "GOOD." When I ask God, "What about me?" God says: "VERY GOOD."

Michael

I know that this sounds funny, but when I think about the first Shabbat, I see an invisible God resting in an endless hammock. God didn't rest from all the work because God was tired. Creating rest was the last job.

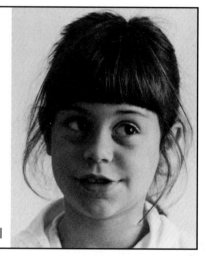

Rachel

Sometimes when I tell the story of creation, I feel like people want me to take a lie detector test. They always want to know if this is a true story. Every story in me is true. Truth is my middle name. What some people don't understand is that there can be a difference between being *true* and being *history*.

BEGINNINGS—A CLOSE LOOK

SECRET MESSAGES

BOOKENDS

One word in this story works like "book-ends." It is in both the first sentence and the last sentence of this story. Look for this word. It will tell you the basic idea of this story. Also, find the other times this word is used in the story. Check your answer on page 210.

MAGIC NUMBER

In this story, God creates things by speaking. **God says: "Let something happen." And it happens**. You can count the number of times God creates in this story by counting the number of times the Torah says: **God said** (Remember to skip the 7 times God says: "GOOD"). Check your answer on page 210.

MAGIC WORDS

GOOD and VERY GOOD טוֹב מְאֹד   טוֹב

When God describes the world, God divides it into two categories: **good** and **very good**. Make your own list of things which are **good** and things which are **very good**.

IN GOD'S IMAGE בְּצֶלֶם אֱלֹהִים

A boy named Levi was talking with his father. The father told Levi that God was invisible.
Levi asked his father: "If God is invisible, can God see God?"
His father thought a long while. He then asked Levi: "When you want to see yourself, where do you look?"
Levi answered his father: "In the mirror."
Then Levi's father said: "When God wants to see God's image, God looks at you, to see it in the best of what you do."

When God is watching you, when would God see **"God's image?"**

This is the family history of the **heavens** and the **earth** from their creation.
On the day when the LORD God made **earth** and **heaven**, there were no bushes and there were no plants growing, because the LORD God had not yet made rain.
There was no HUMAN to till the soil.

CHAPTER 2 **THE GARDEN** Genesis 2.4-25

The LORD God formed ADAM from the **dust** of the **soil** and breathed into his nose the breath of life.
ADAM came alive.

The LORD God planted
a Garden in Eden
and put the HUMAN there.
The LORD God made trees
grow from the soil,
every kind of tree which is
nice to look at and good to eat.
The **TREE OF LIFE** was in
the **middle** of the **garden**
and the TREE OF THE KNOWLEDGE
OF GOOD FROM EVIL.

The LORD God put the HUMAN in
the Garden of Eden,
to work it and to keep it.

The LORD God commanded the HUMAN
"You may eat from every other
tree in the garden
except from the TREE OF
THE KNOWLEDGE OF GOOD FROM EVIL.
You may not eat from it.
Once you eat from it,
you must die."

The LORD God said:
"It is not good that the HUMAN is alone.
I will make a helper who fits with the HUMAN."

So the LORD God formed from the soil
all the wild beasts and all the birds.
And brought each to the HUMAN to see what
the HUMAN would call it.
Whatever the HUMAN called the animal,
that became its name.

But for the HUMAN,
no helper who fit
could be found.

לֹא־טוֹב הֱיוֹת הָאָדָם לְבַדּוֹ

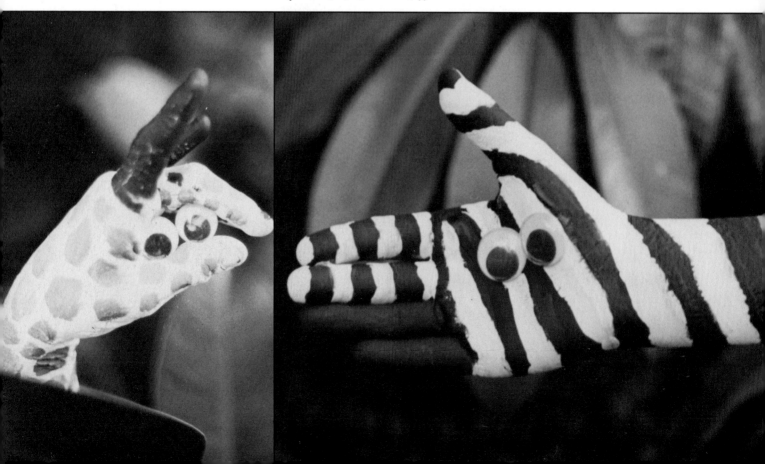

The LORD God made the HUMAN sleep a deep sleep
and took one rib.
The LORD God built the rib into a woman,
and brought her to ADAM.

ADAM said:
"She is the one,
Bone from my bone,
Flesh from my flesh.
She shall be called WO-MAN
because she was taken from MAN."

(This is why a man leaves his father and mother
and clings to his wife
and they become one.)

Now the two of them, ADAM and his wife, were naked,
but they were not embarrassed.

וַיִּהְיוּ לְבָשָׂר אֶחָד

WORDPLAY

Sometimes we can learn a lot from a just a word or two. Because the Torah was written in Hebrew, sometimes we need to look at Hebrew words to find out part of the message.

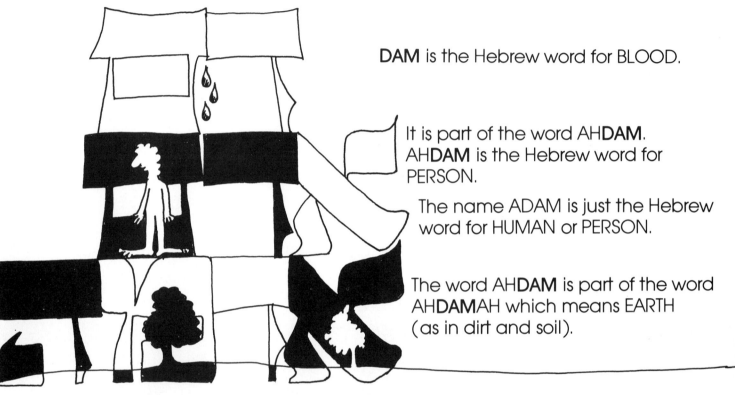

DAM is the Hebrew word for BLOOD.

It is part of the word AH**DAM**. AH**DAM** is the Hebrew word for PERSON.

The name ADAM is just the Hebrew word for HUMAN or PERSON.

The word AH**DAM** is part of the word AH**DAM**AH which means EARTH (as in dirt and soil).

In this story, people are directly connected to the soil.
Look for the places where this happens.

This story also talks about the creation of MAN and WOMAN.

In English, we make the word WOMAN by adding WO to the beginning of the word MAN.

In Hebrew we do it by adding AH to the end of the word EESH.
MAN is EESH.
WOMAN is **EESH**-AH.

EATING THE FRUIT

The snake was the sneakiest
of the animals
which the LORD God had made.
It said to the woman:
"Did God really say that
you may not eat
from any of the trees
in the Garden?"

The woman said to the snake:
"We may eat the fruit from
any of the other trees
in the garden,
but God said:
'The fruit from the **tree**
in the **middle** of the **garden**,
you may not eat it,
and you may not touch it,
or you will die.'"

The snake said to the woman:
"You are not going to die.
Rather, God knows that on the day you eat from it,
your eyes will be opened and you will be like gods,
knowing GOOD from EVIL."

The woman saw that the tree was good for eating
and that it was nice to look at
and that the tree was a source of knowledge.
She took a fruit and ate it.
She gave it to her husband and he ate it.

The eyes of the two of them were opened,
and they knew that they were naked.
They sewed together fig leaves
and made themselves clothing.

EATING THE FRUIT—A CLOSE LOOK

SECRET MESSAGES

FIND THE DIFFERENCE

When God put the HUMAN in the garden, God said:

> "You may eat from every other tree in the garden
> except from the TREE OF THE KNOWLEDGE OF GOOD FROM EVIL.
> You may not eat from it.
> Once you eat from it, you must die."

The snake asked the woman:

> "Did God really say that you may not eat
> from **any of the trees** in the Garden?"

The woman answered the snake:

> "We may eat the fruit from any of the other trees
> in the garden, but God said:
> 'The fruit from the tree in the middle of the garden,
> you may not eat it, **and you may not touch it**,
> or you will die.'"

Can you find what the woman changed? Check your answer on page 210.

LEAVING THE GARDEN

THE GARDEN, Part 3   Genesis 3:9-24

וַיִּקְרָא יְהוָה אֱלֹהִים
אֶל־הָאָדָם
וַיֹּאמֶר לוֹ
אַיֶּכָּה

They heard the sound
of the LORD God
walking around in the Garden
at the windy time of the day.
ADAM and his wife
hid themselves
from the LORD God
in the **middle** of the **trees**
of the **Garden**.

The LORD God called to ADAM
and said to him:
"Where are you?"
He said:
"I heard You in the garden
and I was afraid
because I was naked,
so I hid."

God said:
"Who told you
that you were naked?
Did you eat
from the forbidden tree?"

ADAM said:
"The woman whom You gave me
to be with me—
she gave me from the tree,
and I ate."

28

The LORD God said to the snake: "You shall be cursed.
You shall go on your belly and eat dust
all the days of your life."

God said to the woman: "With pain you will
give birth to children."

And God said to ADAM:
"Because you listened to your wife
and ate from the forbidden tree,
the soil will be cursed because of you.
You will have to sweat and work for your bread
until you return to the **soil** from which you were taken.
For you are **dust** and to **dust** you will return."

Then ADAM called his wife EVE (meaning the life-giver)
because she was going to be the mother of all the living.
The LORD made ADAM and EVE clothing
and dressed them.

The LORD God said: "Now PEOPLE have become like Us,
knowing GOOD from EVIL.
Next, they could take and eat from the TREE OF LIFE
and live forever."

So the LORD GOD sent them away from the Garden of Eden,
to farm the **soil** from which they were taken.
God placed a flaming ever-turning sword
to guard the path to the TREE OF LIFE.

COMMENTARY

I've always imagined that the TREE OF KNOWLEDGE was a kind of library growing out of a tree. It would be this big old oak tree with books growing out of the branches. I've always wanted to climb it, snuggle up on a branch, and just read. I don't know what the TREE OF LIFE looks like.

James

This story always causes trouble. Whenever we read it, the boys and girls always start fighting. The boys all say: "We're better because God made us first." Then the girls say: "No way! God made all the mistakes with the boys. Girls are the new improved model." I always figured that God made Eve out of Adam's side so that the two would be side by side.

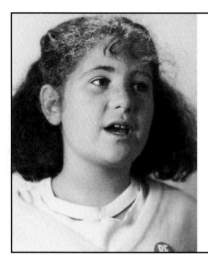

Joanna

I really think that this is just a story about growing up. In the beginning Adam and Eve are like babies. They run around naked in the Garden and God does everything for them. In the end, God dresses them and they have to go to work.

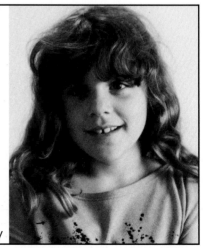

Wendy

THE GARDEN—A CLOSE LOOK

SECRET MESSAGES:

HIDDEN X-PATTERNS

Look at the beginning of this story. Can you see the way the word **heavens** and **earth** make an "X?"

This is the family history of the **heavens** and **earth**

X

On the day when the LORD God made **earth** and **heaven**.

An "x-pattern" is a way of making certain words stand out and be important. In the Torah, it is sort of like an underline.

Find these x-patterns.   Check your answer on page 210.

A.

God said: "The fruit from the _____ in the _____ you shall not eat . . ."

X

ADAM and his wife hid themselves in the _____ of the _____

B.

The LORD God formed ADAM from the _____ of the _____

X

You will have to sweat and work
for your bread until you return to the _____
from which you were taken. For you are _____ and to **dust** you will return.

MAGIC WORDS

WHERE ARE YOU?

A famous rabbi was once thrown in jail by a wicked king. The King's jailer came to see him. The rabbi asked the jailer the same question God asked ADAM. The rabbi asked: **"Where are you?"** The jailer didn't understand. He answered: "I am here in your cell." Then the rabbi asked the jailer: "You are 28 years old, **where are you** in your life?" It was a hard question to answer. The jailer thought a long time, and then said: "I really don't know." In the end, he became a student of the rabbi.

How would you answer this question? **Where are you in your life?**

CHAPTER 3

CAIN AND ABEL Genesis 4.1-26

ADAM knew his wife EVE.
She became pregnant and gave birth to CAIN.
She said: "CAIN means I got a man with God's help"
Later on she gave birth to ABEL, his **brother**.

ABEL became a shepherd.
CAIN farmed the soil.

When time passed,
CAIN brought the fruit of the soil
as a gift-offering for the LORD.
Also ABEL brought the best first-born of his flock.

The LORD accepted ABEL and his gift,
but CAIN and his gift the LORD didn't accept.

CAIN grew angry.
His face fell.

The LORD said to CAIN:
"Why are you angry? Why has your face fallen?
When you are good—aren't you lifted up?
But when you don't do good—
sin haunts your door ready to tempt you.
But YOU can master it."

CAIN said something to his **brother** ABEL.

When they were in the field,
CAIN rose up upon his **brother** ABEL
and killed him.

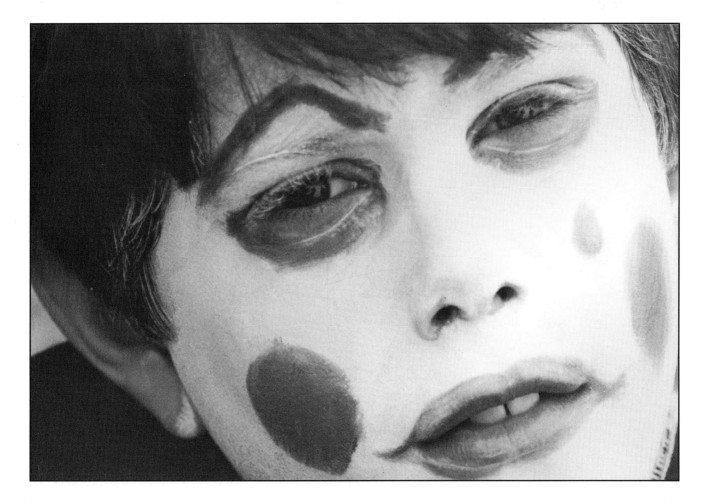

The LORD said to CAIN:
"Where is your **brother** ABEL?"
He said: "I don't know?
Am I my **brother's** keeper?"

הֲשֹׁמֵר אָחִי אָנֹכִי

God said: "What have you done?
The voice of your **brother's** bloods
shouts to Me from the soil.
From now on, you are cursed from the soil
because the soil opened up its mouth
to take your **brother's** bloods from your hand.
From now on, when you farm the soil
it will no longer give you strength.
You will be hunted and wander on the earth."

CAIN: "My punishment is too great.
Whoever meets me may kill me."

The LORD put a mark on CAIN
so whoever met CAIN would know not to kill him.
CAIN left God's presence.
He settled in the land of NOD (meaning the hunted).

COMMENTARY

When I first read this story, I thought that God was really unfair. God seems to be playing favorites. I didn't see any good reason why God should accept Abel's sacrifice and reject Cain's sacrifice. I asked my teacher. She told me to read that part of the story again. The second time I saw the difference. Abel brought *the best of his flock* and Cain just *brought from the fruit of the soil.* Now I know that God wants our best.

David

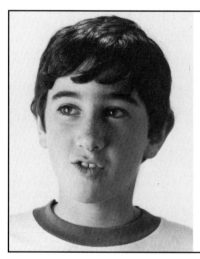

Cain was stupid. God warned him not to act out his anger. God said: "You can control your temper." God said: *"You can master it."* Cain didn't listen. Even though I know better, sometimes I lose my temper, too. What I should do is wait till I calm down before I act—but it doesn't always happen.

Phillip

The big question in this story is *Am I my brother's keeper?* It reminds me of something in the story of Adam and Eve. I looked back to find it. It was part of God's idea of what people can be like. People are supposed to be keepers. In that story it says: *The LORD God put the HUMAN in the Garden to work it and keep it.* Get it?

Stacey

CAIN AND ABEL—A CLOSE LOOK

SECRET MESSAGES

MAGIC SEVENS

It is time to count words again. Count how many times the names CAIN and ABEL are used in this story. Then count how many times the word BROTHER is used. Check your answer on page 210.

AN X-PATTERN

Look at what God says to CAIN. See if you can find the words the x-pattern wants us to notice. Why do you think they are important?

God said: "What have you done?
The voice of your brother's **bloods**
shouts to Me from the **soil**.
From now on, you are cursed from the **soil**
because the soil opened up its mouth
to take your brother's **bloods** from your hand."

The x-pattern is_____and_____,

X

_____and_____.

Check your answer on page 210.

MAGIC WORDS

AM I MY BROTHER'S KEEPER?   הֲשֹׁמֵר אָחִי אָנֹכִי

One of the messages of this story is that people are supposed to be KEEPERS. Make a list of things a person should do to be a good KEEPER of the world.

CHAPTER 4

AND INTRODUCING NOAH Genesis 5.1-6.8

This is family history of ADAM:

When ADAM was
130 years old,
he fathered
SETH.
ADAM lived 930
years.

When SETH was
105 years old,
he fathered
ENOSH.
SETH lived 912
years.

When ENOSH was
90 years old
he fathered
KENAN.
ENOSH lived 905
years.

When KENAN was
70 years old
he fathered
MAHALALEL.
KENAN lived 910
years.

When MAHALALEL
was 65 years old
he fathered
JARED.
MAHALALEL lived
895 years.

When JARED was
162 years old,
he fathered
ENOCH.
JARED lived 962
years.

When ENOCH was
65 years old,
he fathered
METHUSELAH.
ENOCH lived
365 years.

When METHUSELAH
was 187 years
old,
he fathered
LAMECH.
METHUSELAH lived
969 years.

When LAMECH
had lived 182
years, he
fathered a son.
He called his
son NOAH
(which means
the one who
comforts).

LAMECH
explained:
"May he
comfort us
from the pain
of working
the soil which
the LORD
had cursed."

LAMECH lived
777 years.

וְכָל־יֵצֶר מַחְשְׁבֹת לִבּוֹ רַק רַע כָּל־הַיּוֹם

The LORD saw that people did a lot of evil on the earth.
All the thoughts of their hearts
were evil all day long.

The LORD was **uncomfortable** about having made people.
God's heart was pained.
The LORD said:
"I will wipe people off the face of the soil.
I created them:
People,
beasts,
crawling things
and sky birds.
I'm **uncomfortable** that I made them."

But NOAH found favor
in the LORD's eyes.

COMMENTARY

I don't know why the Torah wastes space listing the names of people and then doesn't tell us anything about them. Also, I don't believe that anyone could live 969 years. My grandfather is 71 and he is very old, even if he still walks 2 miles every morning. I don't know . . .

Randy

In my family we get our names from family members who have died. Your name may be a little bit different, but you know that you were named after a great-uncle or a great-grandmother. But Bible-names are like Indian names. Adam was named Adam because God made him out of the *ground*. Eve's name means *"life-giver"* because she was the first mother. And now Noah is named Noah because his father wanted *comfort*. I guess it would have been hard to name Adam after his great-uncle.

Rochelle

INTRODUCING NOAH—A CLOSE LOOK

SECRET MESSAGES:

MAGIC NUMBERS

ADAM was the first HUMAN. In this story, we move from ADAM's family to NOAH's family. Count and find NOAH's number in the family line. (How many generations of people have passed?) Check your answer on page 211.

LIKE PARENT LIKE CHILD

Look at these two verses.

The LORD saw that people did a lot of evil on the earth.
All the **thoughts of their hearts were evil** all day long.

The LORD was uncomfortable about having made people on earth.
God's heart was pained.

What do these two verses teach you about God creating people **"in God's image."** Check your answer on page 211.

FIND THE CHANGE

LAMECH was NOAH's father. He named his son NOAH (which means the comforter). LAMECH explained:

> "May he comfort us from the pain of working the soil which **the LORD had cursed**.

At the end of the story of THE GARDEN, God tells ADAM and EVE.

> "Because you listened to your wife and ate from the forbidden tree, **the ground will be cursed because of you**. You will have to sweat and work for your bread until you return to the soil from which you were taken.

Can you find how LAMECH changed the story? Check your answer on page 211.

A CONNECTION

Look at these two verses. Can you find the secret message?

He called his son NOAH (which means the "one who comforts"). LAMECH explained:

> "May he **comfort** us from the pain of working the soil which the LORD had cursed."

The LORD said:

> "I will wipe people off the face of the soil . . .
> I'm **uncomfortable** that I made them."

> But NOAH found favor in the LORD's eyes.

Check your answer on page 211.

1.

This is the family history of NOAH.
NOAH was a righteous person.
He was the best in his generation.
NOAH walked with God.
NOAH fathered three sons: SHEM, HAM, and JAPHETH.

The earth was being **destroyed** while God watched.
The earth was filled with violence.
God saw the earth—it was **destroyed**,
because each living thing was **destroying**
its way of living.

עֲשֵׂה לְךָ תֵּבָה

2.

God said to NOAH:
"Make yourself a wooden ark.
Make it with rooms and cover it
inside and out with tar.
This is how to make it:
    300 cubits long
      50 cubits wide
      30 cubits high.
Make an opening for light
One cubit below the top.
Make a door in the ark's side.
Make it with a bottom deck,
a second deck,
and a third deck.

As for me,
I am bringing a flood,
but **I will make my covenant**
with you."

3.

The LORD said to NOAH:
"Come into the ark,
you and all your household,
for I have seen that you are
my righteous one
in this generation.

7 days from now
I will make it
rain upon the earth
for 40 days and 40 nights.
I will **wipe off the face of the
earth all the living-things**
that I have made."

4.

NOAH was 600 years old
when the flood came.
**NOAH with his sons,
and his wife,
and his sons' wives,
came into the ark.**
In twos, every kind of living
thing came to NOAH,
to the ark.
They came male and female
just as God commanded him.

5.

7 days later the waters
of the flood
were over the earth.
All the waters came up from
the deepest places.
The floodgates of the sky
broke open.
The rain fell on the earth
40 days and 40 nights.

Two of every kind of living
thing were in the ark with
NOAH, just as God had
commanded.

Then, **the LORD shut him in.**

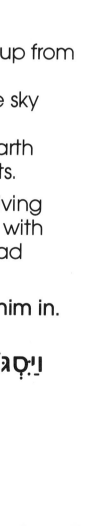

וַיִּסְגֹּר יהוה בַּעֲדוֹ

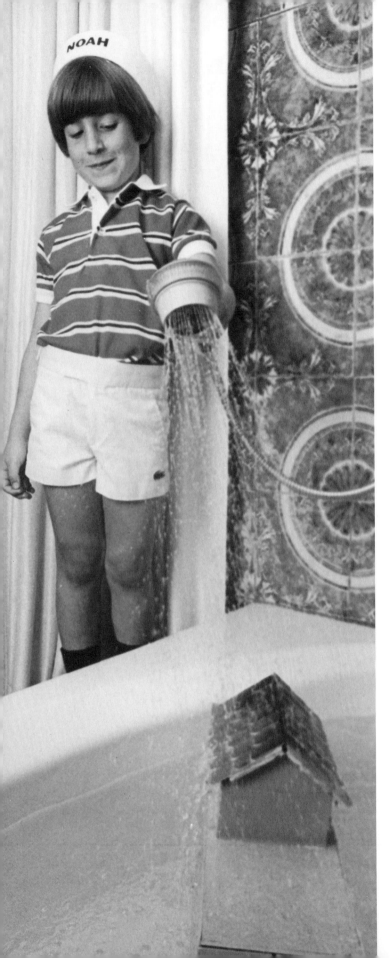

6.

The flood continued
for 40 days.
The waters grew
and lifted the ark.
The waters swelled and grew
and the ark went
on the face of the waters.
The waters swelled
very very much
and **all the high mountains
were covered**.

Everything
that had the breath of life,
everything
that was on dry land, died.

Only NOAH survived,
and those with him in the ark.

The waters swelled
for 150 days.

וַיְהִי הַגֶּשֶׁם עַל־הָאָרֶץ
אַרְבָּעִים יוֹם וְאַרְבָּעִים לָיְלָה

COMMENTARY

When I imagine going on the ark, I imagine bringing two teddy bears (male and female).

Loren

I really wonder what it must have been like to be the only righteous kid in your school. For me, it is hard enough being one of the few Jewish kids in my school. Noah's kids must have had a really hard time. They were a real minority.

Ellen

The thing which really surprises me in this story is the one sentence that tells us that God closed the ark door. In this story, Noah is the world's keeper. God gives him the responsibility and makes him do all the work. Of course, he has his family, and they help to build the ark and gather the animals. Only after Noah and his family have worked hard to do what God asked does God help out. In the end, God shows Noah that people are not alone. That makes me feel good. Even if being the world's keepers means we have to work hard to fix it, maybe God will help us in the end.

Jon

CUBIT DEPARTMENT

Like a foot, a cubit was an ancient measurement. In those days a foot was measured by the size of someone's foot. A cubit was the distance from a grown-up man's elbow to the tip of his index finger. Later, people decided that every foot measured by a builder needed to be the same size. They picked a size and called it a foot. They did the same thing with a cubit.

TRY IT OUT

1. Take a string, find an adult and measure a cubit.
2. Measure your height in cubits. Use your string as a ruler. You may want to fold it to make a half-cubit or a quarter-cubit.
3. Measure your room in cubits.

HALF-TIME WORK-OUT

The NOAH story is a long story, but it was written very carefully. Here is one thing to look for in the second half of the story.

In the first-half of the story:

> NOAH and his family wait **7 days** in the ark.
> It rains for **40 days** and **40 nights**.
> The water rises for **150 days**.

When you read the second-half of the story, watch the number of days things take.

7.

God remembered NOAH and all the living things
and all the animals that were with him in the ark.
God brought a breath of wind across the earth
and the waters went down.
The rain from the sky stopped.
The waters **returned** from covering the earth.
They were constantly moving and **returning**.
After 150 days, there was less water.
The ark came to rest on the mountains of Ararat.
The tops of the mountains could be seen.

וַיִּזְכֹּר אֱלֹהִים אֶת־נֹחַ

After 40 days,
NOAH opened the window
in the ark and sent out a raven.
The raven kept
leaving and **returning**
until the waters were dried up.

Then he sent out a dove
to see if there was still water
on the the face of the soil.
But the dove could not find
a place to rest her feet
so she **returned** to him.
(The waters were still on the
face of all the earth.)
He stuck out his hand
and took her
and brought her into the ark.
He waited another 7 days
and again sent the dove
from the ark.
The dove came to him
in the evening.
In her beak there were
fresh olive leaves.
This is how NOAH knew
that the waters had gone down.
He waited 7 days,
sent out the dove,
but she **returned** no more.
When NOAH took off
the covering to the ark,
he saw that
the face of the soil was drying.
Soon the earth was dry.

8.

God spoke to NOAH:
"Go out of the ark.
Bring out all the living things
that are with you—
all life: birds, animals,
and all crawling things,
that they can be fruitful
and become many on the earth."

9.

So NOAH went out,
and his sons
and his wife
and his sons' wives.
All living things
came out of the ark by families.

NOAH built an altar to the LORD.
He burned sacrifices on the altar.
The LORD smelled
the pleasing smell
and the LORD thought:
I will NEVER AGAIN curse the soil
because of people.
I will NEVER AGAIN wipe out
all living things.
NEVER AGAIN
in all the earth's days
    will seeding time
    and harvest time
    cold and heat
    summer and winter
    day and night
come to end."

10.

God blessed NOAH and his sons, saying:
    "Be fruitful
    and become many
    and fill the earth.
Every living moving thing shall be for your eating.
Just like the green plants I now give you all to eat.
But you must not eat the living, bloody flesh.

And also for your blood, I will seek responsibility
from every person for the life of her brother or sister.
Whoever sheds the BLOOD of a **person**
by a **person** shall his BLOOD be shed,
because God created people in God's image.

Be fruitful
and become many
and **fill the earth**
and become many on it."

11.

God said to NOAH and to his sons with him:
"**As for Me, I now make my covenant with you**
and with your family after you
and with every living-thing that was with you.
I will make my **covenant** with you.

NEVER AGAIN will all life be wiped out
by the waters of a flood.
NEVER AGAIN will there be a flood
to destroy the earth."

12

Then God said:
"This is sign of the **covenant**
that I give between Me and you,
and with all the living-things
with you
for all generations to come.

I give my rainbow in the clouds
which will be
the sign of the **covenant**
between Me and the earth.

Whenever I cloud the skies
with clouds—
whenever a rainbow appears
in those clouds—
I will remember My **covenant**.

NEVER AGAIN
will waters become a flood
to destroy all life.

When the rainbow
is in the clouds
I will look at it and remember
my everlasting **covenant**."

God said to NOAH:

"That is the sign of
the **covenant**."

וְנִרְאֲתָה הַקֶּשֶׁת בֶּעָנָן
וְזָכַרְתִּי אֶת־בְּרִיתִי

COMMENTARY

This story is like a new creation story. In the first creation story, one family has to fill the world. In the Noah story, a new family has to again fill the world. The first story begins with a breath of wind from God blowing over the water. The flood begins to end when God blows a breath of wind over the flood-waters. I like that.

Stephanie

Udeka

There is something in this story that makes me feel two different ways. The flood began to end when God *remembered* Noah. I like the idea that God remembers. That means that God might remember us, too. It also scares me that God might forget.

NOAH—A CLOSE LOOK

SECRET MESSAGES

MAGIC NUMBERS

In the last half of this story (parts 11 and 12) one word is used 7 times. This word changes the partnership between God and people. Find this word. Check your answer on page 211.

FIND THE DIFFERENCE

In the second half of this story, God rebuilds the world. Like ADAM and EVE, God gives commands to NOAH and his family. Can you find the difference between these commands and those in chapter 1?

God said to ADAM and EVE:
>"Be fruitful, and become many,
>and fill the earth and master it."

God said to NOAH and his family:
>"Be fruitful, and become many
>and fill the earth."

Check your answer on page 211.

MAGIC WORDS

THE BEST IN HIS GENERATION   תָּמִים הָיָה בְּדֹרֹתָיו

The Torah begins the NOAH story by telling us what made NOAH special. It says: **NOAH was a righteous person. He was the best in his generation. NOAH walked with God.** Imagine walking with NOAH for a day. What do you think he would do to show you that he is a righteous person?

The prophet Micah said that God expects a good person do three things: (1) Seek justice, (2) Love mercy, and (3) walk with God. The Torah says that **NOAH walked with God.** What do you think it means to "walk with God?"

WHEN A RAINBOW APPEARS   וְהָיְתָה הַקֶּשֶׁת בֶּעָנָן וּרְאִיתִיהָ לִזְכֹּר

After the flood, God made a rainbow as a reminder of the covenant with NOAH. God says: **Whenever I cloud the skies with clouds—whenever a rainbow appears in those clouds—I will remember My covenant.** Do you think that the rainbow is just a reminder for God?

GOD CREATED PEOPLE IN GOD'S IMAGE   בְּצֶלֶם אֱלֹהִים עָשָׂה אֶת־הָאָדָם

A famous rabbi went to ancient Rome during the winter. There he saw a Roman wrapping the statues in rugs and blankets to keep them warm. This Roman passed by beggars and poor people living in the streets. They had only rags to keep them warm. The rabbi said: "The Roman remembers to care for images of himself, but forgets to care for God's image." What did the Rabbi mean?

וְנַעֲשֶׂה־לָּנוּ שֵׁם

CHAPTER 5

THE TOWER OF BABEL

Genesis 11.1-9

(1) **All the earth** had one **language**
and used one set of words.
(2) People traveled to the east
and found a valley in the Land of Shinar
and settled **there**.
(3) **People** said **to their neighbors**:
"**OKAY, let us** make bricks and burn them hard."
(For them bricks were stones.
For them tar was cement.)
(4) Then they said: "OKAY, let us **build** a **city**
and a **tower** with its top in the sky.
Let us make a name for ourselves,
to keep us from being scattered
over the face of all the earth."
(5) The LORD came down to see the **city** and the **tower**
that ADAM's children were building.
(6) The LORD said: "Now, they are one people
with one language.
This is only the beginning of what they will do.
From now on, they will be able to do whatever
they feel like doing.
(7) **OKAY, let us** go down and babble their language
so that **people** will not understand
their **neighbors'** language."
(8) So the LORD scattered them from **there**
over the face of all the earth
and they stopped building the city.
(9) That is why the city is called Babel,
because there the LORD babbled
the **language** of **all the earth**.
And from there, the LORD scattered them
over the face of all the earth.

COMMENTARY

These stories are all the same. Adam and Eve do wrong and God punishes them. Cain does wrong and God punishes him. People are evil and God punishes the world with a flood. This story is about another punishment.

Adam

Wrong! When you are a parent, you've got to expect kids to make mistakes. Every one of these stories is about God setting people on the right path.

Andrea

In this story, people start out working together and cooperating. Then God breaks them up so that no one can understand anyone else. Today, people complain that different countries don't understand each other. It seems to me that this is God's fault.

Joanna

You read this story and the first question you ask is: "What is wrong with building a tower?" You think that God was afraid that the tower would reach heaven? I don't think that was the problem. God must have seen something wrong in the way people were working on the tower. The people wanted to make a name for themselves. I think they must have tried too hard to be famous.

Michael

THE TOWER OF BABEL—A CLOSE LOOK

SECRET MESSAGES

SECRET PLANS

The story of the **Tower of Babel** is the story of a building. When we look at the way the story is "built," we can find the patterns for two different buildings. We can see a pyramid and a sky-scraper.

THE PYRAMID

Look at this story and fill in the second side to this pyramid.

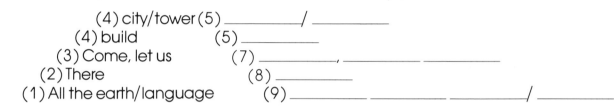

```
        (4) city/tower (5) _____ / _____
         (4) build          (5) _____
        (3) Come, let us      (7) _____, _____ _____
       (2) There               (8) _____
   (1) All the earth/language    (9) _____ _____ _____ / _____
```

Can you find the **x-pattern** which works as book-ends for this story? Check your answer on page 212.

THE SKY-SCRAPER

The second pattern for this story is like a tall building. In a sky-scraper, all the floors are built using the same pattern. In this story, we are shown two floors. On the bottom floor we see people's actions. On the top floor we see God's reaction. Find the correct letters to fill the blanks in each sentence.

A. one language **B.** Come, let us **C** build/city **D1** there (sham) **D2** name (shem)
E. scattered/over/face of the earth

(God's Actions)

(6) Now they are one people with _____ _____
(7) _____, _____ _____ go down there and babble
(8) The LORD babbled the language of all the earth. And from _____.
(9) The LORD _____ them _____ the _____ _____ _____ _____.

(People's Actions)

(1) All the earth was _____ _____.
(3) People said to their neighbors, "_____, _____ _____ make bricks."
(4) Then they said: "Come, let us _____ a _____.
(4) Let us make a _____ for ourselves.
(4) So we won't be _____ _____ the _____ _____ _____ _____."

Check your answer on Page 212.

59

Chapter 6

AND INTRODUCING ABRAM Genesis 11.10-26

NOAH fathered 3 sons: SHEM, HAM and JAPHETH.
This is the family history of SHEM.

SHEM fathered ARPACHSHAD 2 years after the flood.
ARPACHSHAD fathered SHELAH.
SHELAH fathered EBER.
EBER fathered PELEG.
PELEG fathered REU.
REU fathered SERUG.
SERUG fathered NAHOR.
NAHOR fathered TERAH.
TERAH fathered **ABRAM**, NAHOR, and HARAN.

This is the family history of TERAH.
TERAH fathered ABRAM, NAHOR and HARAN.
HARAN fathered LOT.
HARAN died while his father
was still living in Ur of the Chaldeans.
Both ABRAM and NAHOR married.
ABRAM's wife was named SARAI.
NAHOR was married to MILCAH.
SARAI had no children.

TERAH took ABRAM his son
and LOT his grandson
and SARAI, ABRAM's wife.
Together they left Ur of the Chaldeans
to go to the land of Canaan.
They went as far as Haran and settled there.
TERAH lived 205 years.
TERAH died in HARAN.

COMMENTARY

This story is like the clues in a mystery. We know what happens, we don't know why. Terah and part of his family leave Ur to go Canaan. We don't know why they left. They only go as far as Haran. We don't know why they stopped. Sometimes the Torah has more questions than answers.

Kenny

Before I ever read the Bible, I used to think that it was just a story book. My mother was really into genealogy. That is where you make a tree of the whole family. She's no longer that interested, but we still have this big chart in the den which shows who married whom and who were their kids all the way back to 1823. The stories inside the Bible are the same thing. It is really a book of family history. Between every story you get a list of who married whom and who were their kids.

Scott

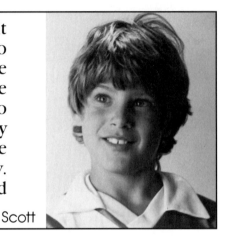

INTRODUCING ABRAM—A CLOSE LOOK

SECRET MESSAGES

MAGIC NUMBERS

Count how many generations there are from SHEM (NOAH's son) to ABRAM. Where have we seen this number before? Check your answer on page 212.

MYSTERY

Up to now the Torah has told us only short stories. Each story was about new people. The Torah is now going to tell us many stories about ABRAM and SARAI. What do we know about their childhood? Check your answer on page 212.

CHAPTER 7

ABRAM: LEAVING HOME Genesis 12.1-7

לֶךְ־לְךָ מֵאַרְצְךָ וּמִמּוֹלַדְתְּךָ וּמִבֵּית אָבִיךָ
אֶל־הָאָרֶץ אֲשֶׁר אַרְאֶךָּ

The LORD said to ABRAM:
"Take yourself,
from your **land**,
from your birthplace,
from your father's house,
to the **land**: there I will let you **see**.

(1) And I will make you a great nation
(2) And I will BLESS you.
(3) And I will make your name great.
(4) And you will be a BLESSING.
(5) And I will BLESS those who BLESS you.
(6) (And I will curse anyone who curses you)—
(7) All the families of the earth will be BLESSED through you.

ABRAM went as the LORD had told him,
and LOT went with him.
ABRAM was 75 years old when he left Haran.

ABRAM took SARAI his wife,
and LOT his nephew,
and all they owned,
and all their people,
and they left for the **land** of Canaan.

The came to the **land** of Canaan.
ABRAM crossed the **land**
as far as Shechem.
(The Canaanites then lived in the **land**.)
The LORD was **seen** by ABRAM.
The LORD said:
"To your future-family I will give this **land**."

ABRAM built an altar
to the LORD Who is **seen** by him.

וַיִּבֶן שָׁם מִזְבֵּחַ לַיהוה הַנִּרְאֶה אֵלָיו

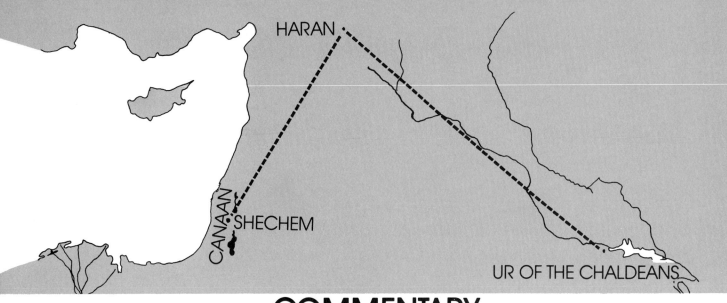

HARAN

CANAAN • SHECHEM

UR OF THE CHALDEANS

COMMENTARY

In this story God makes a big deal out of telling Abram to leave home. You get the feeling that Abram had to be a pioneer to boldly go where no one had gone before—like Daniel Boone or Christopher Columbus or an astronaut. When I said that in class, my teacher said that lots of people used to go from Haran to Canaan. It was a highway for caravans. She said: "Abram was a pioneer because he went looking for God." I never heard of that kind of pioneer.

Mara

So far, God blessed Adam and Eve, God blessed Noah. Now, God blesses Abram. At my house we "bless" people when they sneeze. I guess we are wishing that they get better. And our rabbi blesses the congregation from the bima with wishes for peace and stuff. But I don't know anyone who goes around giving or getting blessings. What is all this blessing business?

Dani

LEAVING HOME—A CLOSE LOOK

SECRET MESSAGES

MAGIC NUMBERS

Count how many times **ABRAM's** name is used. Then count how many times the word **land** is used. Now count the number of lines in the BLESSING that God gives to ABRAM. What do you think this all means? Check your answer on page 212.

A SECRET CONNECTION

People always ask: "Why did ABRAM leave his home to go to the land which God commanded." There is no one right answer. See if you can find a good answer by looking at these two sentences. Check your answer on page 212.

The LORD said to ABRAM: "Take yourself from your land,
from your birthplace, from your father's house
to the land: there I will let you **see**."

They came to the land of Canaan.
ABRAM crossed the **land** as far as Shechem.
The LORD was **seen** by ABRAM.

MAGIC WORDS

TAKE YOURSELF FROM YOUR LAND, FROM YOUR BIRTHPLACE, FROM YOUR FATHER'S HOUSE   לֶךְ־לְךָ

If God told you to leave everything behind and go to a new place. Which would you miss most—your home, your neighborhood, or your country?

AND YOU WILL BE A BLESSING   וֶהְיֵה בְּרָכָה

Jews make blessings. We say blessings when we drink wine, light candles and eat challah. Usually our blessings thank God, and help us to remember that we are doing something special. We know how to make blessings, but what does it mean to be a blessing? How could your parents call you a blessing?

A VISIT TO EGYPT

We are not going to study the text of the next story. We are just going to tell you what happens! People are starving in the land of Canaan. ABRAM and his family go down to Egypt to get food. In Egypt, PHARAOH (the king of Egypt), sees SARAI and falls in love with her. He doesn't know that SARAI is married to ABRAM. When PHARAOH learns that SARAI is married, he sends her back to ABRAM. Then ABRAM, SARAI and the family return to Canaan. This is where we pick up the text.

CHAPTER 8 **ABRAM: LOT LEAVES** Genesis 13.1-18

ABRAM went up from Egypt.
He and his wife, and all that was his.
And LOT went with him.
ABRAM was very rich in herds, in silver, and in gold.
And LOT (who went with ABRAM)
also owned sheep, oxen, and tents.

כִּי־אֲנָשִׁים אַחִים אֲנָחְנוּ׃

The **land** would not support
both of them SETTLING together.
They had so many belongings that they
were not able to SETTLE together.

There was feuding between
ABRAM's herdsmen and LOT's herdsmen.
(At that time, the Canaanites and the Perizzites
were SETTLED in the **land**).
ABRAM said to LOT:
"Let there be no feud between me and you,
between my herdsmen and between your herdsmen,
because we are **men** who are like **brothers**.
The whole **land** is before you—please DIVIDE from me.
If you go to the left, I will go to the right.
If you go the right, I will go to the left."

LOT lifted up his eyes and saw
the plain of the Jordan.
It was **land** with much water.
LOT chose the Jordan plain
and journeyed eastward.

So they were DIVIDED—
each **man** from his **brother**.

ABRAM SETTLED
in the **land** of Canaan.
LOT SETTLED
in the cities of the plain
and pitched his tents
near Sodom.

The men of Sodom
were evil
and sinned on purpose.

The LORD said to ABRAM
after LOT was DIVIDED from
him:
"Lift up your eyes
and look around.

North,
South,
East and
West.
All the **land** which you see,
I give it to you
and to your future-family
forever.

Your future-family will be
like dust covering the **land**.
Like the dust of the **land**,—
Your future-family will be
impossible to count.

Get up and walk the **land**
from end to end
and from side to side—
because I give it to you."

ABRAM moved his tents
and SETTLED near Hebron.
There he built an altar to
the LORD.

וְשַׂמְתִּי אֶת־זַרְעֲךָ
כַּעֲפַר הָאָרֶץ

70

COMMENTARY

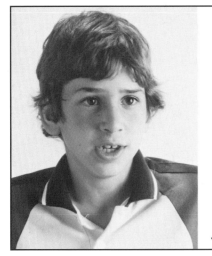

Why do families have to fight? People should get along. Especially families. It seems stupid for Abram and Lot to split up. They were both strangers in Canaan. And they were the only family for each other. I think they should have stayed together and worked out their problems.

Jordan

When I read this story, I wonder where Sarai is? They don't say anything about her feelings about Lot leaving. She was his aunt. Then Abram goes off and talks to God about the future. She should have been included.

Amy

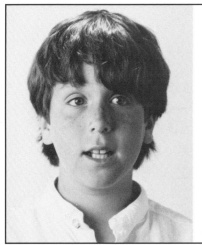

Lot made a bad decision. When he left Abram he made a bad choice. We can already tell that he is going to get in trouble in Sodom. The people living there sound terrible. When you decide to live somewhere, you've got to think about who your neighbors will be.

Jeff

ABRAM: LOT LEAVES—A CLOSE LOOK

SECRET MESSAGES

FIND THE CHANGE

Can you find the difference between the way that ABRAM's family first arrived in Canaan and the way the family returned to Canaan from Egypt.

Arriving in Canaan

> ABRAM took SARAI his wife, and LOT his brother's son and **all they owned**.

Returning from Egypt

> ABRAM went up from Egypt. He and his wife, and **all that was his**. And LOT went with him . . . also owned sheep, oxen and tents.

HINT: Keep your eyes on who owns what. That is an important clue for understanding this story. Check your answer on page 212.

REPEATED WORDS

There are no "magic numbers" in this story, but two important words are repeated many times. Can you find them? Check your answer on page 212.

TWO PART PROMISE

After LOT leaves, God makes a promise with two parts to ABRAM.

(1) All the land which you see _____ .
(2) I will make your family as _____ as _____ .

Go back to chapter 7, LEAVING HOME and see if you can find the same two promises in that story. Check your answer on page 213.

MAGIC WORDS

BECAUSE WE ARE MEN—WHO ARE LIKE BROTHERS   כִּי־אֲנָשִׁים אַחִים אֲנָחְנוּ

In the story of CAIN and ABEL we learn that people are supposed to be their **brother's keepers**. When ABRAM called LOT his **brother**, he wasn't talking only about a family relationship. They were uncle and nephew. ABRAM was saying that the two of them should act like **brothers—keeping** each other. At the end of the story it is sad that they have to split-up. Families are often forced to split-up. There are divorces, deaths, moves to other cities and all kinds of causes. It is usually sad, but sometimes this helps us to grow. What are some ways a split-up is sad? What are some ways that split-ups help us to grow?

A WAR STORY

Here we skip another story. This one is a war story. Four kings come into Canaan from other lands. They make war against 5 cities ruled by Canaanite kings and defeat them. The four kings capture all the wealth of Sodom and kidnap LOT.

One person escapes and tells ABRAM, who gathers together his 318 men and chases the 4 kings. ABRAM wins, frees Lot, and returns all the stolen money and captured prisoners. Our text goes on right after this story.

CHAPTER 9 **ABRAM: A COVENANT** Genesis 15.1-24

After these things
the LORD's word came to ABRAM
in a vision saying:
"Don't be afraid ABRAM.
I am your shield.
Your reward is very great."

ABRAM said:
"My Master the LORD,
what could You give me?
I have no children.
The only 'son' in my household
is my servant Dammesek Eliezer."

ABRAM also said:
"Up to NOW you've given me no **future-family**.
Up to NOW, Eliezer will **inherit** from me."

אָנֹכִי מָגֵן לָךְ שְׂכָרְךָ הַרְבֵּה מְאֹד

And NOW the LORD's word
came to him:
"This one will not
inherit from you.
Only your own children will
inherit from you."

The LORD took him outside
and said:
"Look toward the sky.
Count the stars,
if you can count them.
This is the number
of your **future-family**."

ABRAM trusted in the LORD
and the LORD gave him credit
for being righteous.

The LORD said to him:
"I am the LORD
who brought you out from
Ur of the Chaldeans
to give this land
for you to **inherit**".
ABRAM said:
"My Master the LORD,
How do I know that I will
inherit it?"

וּסְפֹר הַכּוֹכָבִים אִם־תּוּכַל
לִסְפֹּר אֹתָם

The LORD said to him: "Take a 3 year old calf,
a 3 year old goat, a 3 year old ram,
a dove and a baby pigeon,
and divide them for Me as a sacrifice."

When the sun was setting, a deep sleep fell on ABRAM.
And NOW, a deep dark fear covered him.

The LORD said to ABRAM: "Know for a fact
that your **future-family** will be strangers
in a land which is not theirs.
They shall be slaves and suffer for 400 years.
But I will punish the nation they serve,
and after that, they will exit with riches."

When the sun set, there was a deep darkness.
And NOW, a smoking furnace and a flaming torch
which passed through the sacrifice.

On that day, the LORD cut a covenant with ABRAM.
The LORD said: "I will give this land
to your **future-family**."

COMMENTARY

Wow, is Abram patient! He sure knows a lot about waiting. God keeps promising him a big family and a land of his own. While God keeps making promises, Abram and Sarai have no children and they are living like nomads, camping all over Canaan. Somehow, Abram is happy. When my mother makes me a promise, I bug her till she keeps it. Sometimes I even make her put it in writing. Abram is satisfied to wait with a handful of dust and a look at the sky.

Jeff

In chapter 8, LOT LEAVES, God says to Abram: "You'll have as many future-family members as their are pieces of dust in the world." In this story, God says: "You'll have as many future-family members as there are stars." I drew this cartoon of Abram sitting in a sandbox. He is picking up a grain of sand and saying: "North Star." Then he picks up another grain of sand and says: "Alpha Centauri." No one in my class understood it, but Ms. Seglin liked it.

Sam

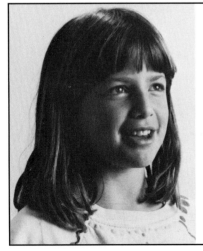

This story comes from the Twilight Zone. Abram has a weird vision at sundown, and God predicts that the Jewish people will be slaves in the land of Egypt. It's kind of spooky.

Andrea

WORDPLAY

When we think of a family, we usually think of our living family—mother, father, children; and sometimes grandparents, cousins, uncles, aunts, and the rest. When ABRAM talks to God about his family, he talks about his future-family. Generation after generation. The Torah uses the Hebrew word זֶרַע **Zera** which means seed. A seed holds the beginning of a new living plant. When that plant grows, it produces new seeds which produce new plants, generation after generation. Scientists teach us that HUMAN genes do the same thing—they are like seeds that we pass on through our future-family.

ABRAM: A COVENANT—A CLOSE LOOK

SECRET MESSAGES

REPEATED WORDS

In this story there are 2 important repeated words. They stand for the 2 promises God makes to ABRAM. Find these 2 words. Check your answer on page 213.

TWO PART PROMISE

At the end of chapter 8, LOT LEAVES, God makes two promises to ABRAM. So far, neither promise has come true. In this story, ABRAM questions those two promises. Find the two questions ABRAM asks. Check your answer on page 213.

WORD ECHOES

In chapter 8, LOT LEAVES, God promises ABRAM: **"Like the dust of the land your future-family will be impossible to count."** Look back at chapter 2, THE GARDEN. Find out how the words **dust** and **soil** are used there.

In this story, God says to ABRAM: **"Count the stars, if you can count them. This is the number of your future-family."** Look at chapter 1, BEGINNINGS, and see what it says about what stars do. Here is a clue: Look at the 4th day. Check your answers on page 213.

MAGIC WORDS

I AM YOUR SHIELD   אָנֹכִי מָגֵן לָךְ

In this story, God promises to be a shield for ABRAM. A shield protects us from danger. How do you think God protected ABRAM? How does God protect you?

יָדֹעַ תֵּדַע כִּי־גֵר יִהְיֶה זַרְעֲךָ בְּאֶרֶץ לֹא לָהֶם
KNOW FOR A FACT THAT YOUR FUTURE-FAMILY WILL BE STRANGERS . . . .

In the book of EXODUS, ABRAM's future-family will become strangers in a land not theirs—in Egypt, just as God predicts here. Because they will be **strangers**, the Egyptians will make them slaves. What does it feel like to be a **stranger**? What would it feel like to be a **stranger** with a **shield**?

ABRAM'S FIRST BORN SON

This time we are skipping a story where ABRAM fathers a son named ISH-MAEL. The mother was a servant named HAGAR.

SARAI was sad that she had not given birth to any children. She wanted ABRAM to have a family. She did something that was a custom in those days, but that we wouldn't do today. She asked ABRAM to take HAGAR as a secondary-wife.

When she is pregnant, HAGAR begins to tease SARAI about being childless. SARAI complains to ABRAM, but ABRAM reminds SARAI that HAGAR is her servant. ABRAM tells SARAI to do as she wishes. SARAI is cruel to HAGAR, who runs away into the desert. There she meets an angel who tells her that she is pregnant with a son whose future-family will be a great nation. The angel tells her to name her son ISHMAEL. ISHMAEL means God listens. HAGAR goes back to camp and gives birth to her son.

CHAPTER 10 **ABRAM BECOMES ABRAHAM** Genesis 17:1-27

1.

When ABRAM was 99 years old
the LORD appeared to ABRAM
and said to him:
"I am God SHADDAI,
Walk before me
and be **the best**.

I put my **covenant**
between Me and you.
I will make you very,
very many."

79

2.

ABRAM bowed to the ground.
God spoke with him:
"As for me
HERE—my **covenant** is with you.
You will become the
father of many nations.
No longer will your name be
called ABRAM.
Instead your name
will be ABRAHAM
for I will make you
AV HAMON GOYYIM
(the father of many nations).
Many nations and rulers
will come from you.

I set up my **covenant**
for Me and for you
and for your **future-family**
after you.
It is an EVERLASTING **covenant**.
I will be God to you
and to your **future-family**.

I will give to you
and to your **future-family**,
the land where you are staying.
All the land of Canaan will be
yours FOREVER."

כִּי אַב־הֲמוֹן גּוֹיִם נְתַתִּיךָ

3.

God said to ABRAHAM
"As for you,
you are to keep my **covenant**,
You and your **future-family**.
This is my **covenant**—
Circumcise every male.
That will be the sign
of the **covenant**
between me and between you.
When he is eight days old,
every one of your boys
should be circumcised."

4.

God said to ABRAHAM:
"As for SARAI your wife—
don't call her SARAI anymore,
because SARAH is now her name.
I will bless her
and I will give you a son
from her.
I will bless her
and nations and rulers
will come from her."

ABRAHAM fell to the ground
laughing. He thought:
"How is a 100-year-old man
going to father a son?
How is 90-year-old SARAH
going to give birth?"

ABRAHAM said to God:
"If only ISHMAEL
would live before you . . . "

God said:
"SARAH, your wife, will yet
give birth to a son.
You will name him ISAAC
(meaning he laughs).
I will set up my **covenant**
with him
as an EVERLASTING **covenant**.

As for ISHMAEL—I hear you.
I bless him.
I make him fruitful.
I make him very very many.
He will father 12 princes.
I will make a great nation
of him.

But my **covenant**
I will set up with ISAAC."

When God finished speaking
with him
God went up from ABRAHAM.

5.

ABRAHAM took ISHMAEL his son
and all the males
among ABRAHAM's household
and circumcised them.
ABRAHAM was 99 years old
when he was circumcised.
ISHMAEL was 13 years old
when he was circumcised.
On that very day,
ABRAHAM, ISHMAEL his son,
and all of his household were
circumcised.

COMMENTARY

I got embarrassed by this chapter. You're not supposed to talk about things like circumcision. It has no business being in the Torah, and they shouldn't make us study it in a Jewish school.

Danny

What's so bad about talking about circumcision? It's just an operation, and as far as Jewish school goes they should teach it, because it is the first symbol of the covenant which God made with Israel.

Brittany

Well here we go, God is still making more promises to Abraham. We get the same two promises—a big family and a land. God still hasn't delivered on God's side of the covenant. But Abraham is now expected to act on his side of the deal. Maybe that's the message. People have to do something themselves in order for God's promises to come true.

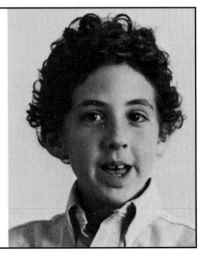

Michael

WORDPLAY

In Hebrew ABRAM's name is אַבְרָם AV-RAM. It could mean "honored father."

AV-RA-HAM is the new name God gives him. It comes from AV HAMON GOYYIM, which means father of many nations. ABRAHAM is already the father of ISHMAEL, who will father many nations. Soon ISAAC, the next father of the Jewish people, will be born. This name will come true. In one way, this name also completes one promise God made to ABRAM. God said: **"I will make your name great."** How does changing ABRAM to ABRAHAM make this promise come true?

God also changes SARAI's name to SARAH. No one knows for sure what this change means. Both names mean "princess."

ABRAM BECOMES ABRAHAM—A CLOSE LOOK

SECRET MESSAGES

MAGIC NUMBER

One name in this story is used 10 times. Find out whose name it is? Check your answer on page 213.

FIND THE CONNECTION

In chapter 9, A COVENANT, the Torah says: **ABRAM trusted in the LORD and the LORD gave him credit for being righteous.** In this story, the Torah says: **The LORD appeared to ABRAM and said to him: " . . . Walk before Me and be the best."** Find the other person whom the Torah describes as being **righteous**, **the best**, and **walking** with God. Check your answer on page 213.

In this story, God tells ABRAHAM to **keep** the covenant. This is the third time that God has told us to be **keepers**. Can you find the other two? (Look in chapter 2, THE GARDEN and chapter 3, CAIN AND ABEL). Check your answer on page 213.

CHAPTER 11

SARAH LAUGHED Genesis 18.1-15

Now the LORD appeared to ABRAHAM.
He was sitting at the entrance of the tent
during the heat of the day.
He lifted his eyes and saw.
And SUDDENLY three men were standing over him.
He saw them and **ran** toward them.

He bowed to the ground and said: "My masters,
please, if I have found favor in your eyes,
please do not pass by me.
Please let me bring you a little water.
Wash your feet and rest under the tree.
Let me bring you some bread."
They said: "Do just what you have said."

ABRAHAM **hurried** into SARAH's tent.
He said: "**Hurry**
Three measures of good flour—
Knead it and bake bread."

ABRAHAM **ran** to the herd.
He took a tender calf
and gave it to a servant,
so that he could **hurry** to prepare it.

He took yogurt and milk
and the calf which had been cooked,
and served it to them.
He stood by them under the tree
while they ate.

They said to him: "Where is SARAH, your wife?"
And he said: "RIGHT HERE, in the tent."
One said:
"I will definitely return at the time of birth,
when SARAH your wife will have a son."

SARAH was listening at the entrance to the tent.
ABRAHAM and SARAH were old.
SARAH was too old to have a child.

SARAH **laughed** and said to herself:
"Now that my time has passed,
how can my old husband and I have a child?"

וַיֹּאמֶר לֹא כִּי צָחָקְתְּ

The LORD said to ABRAHAM:
"Why is SARAH laughing and saying:
'Will I really give birth, now that I am old?'
Is any miracle too great for the LORD?
I will return to you at the time of birth,
when SARAH will have a son."

SARAH denied it: "I did not laugh."
She was afraid.
She was answered: "You did so laugh."

COMMENTARY

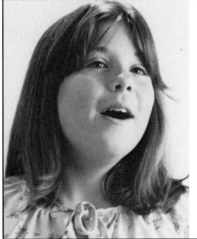

This story is the one that really makes you think that Abraham was like a desert sheik. You see his tents, his clay oven, his servants, and all his cattle. He goes and asks people who are passing by to be his guests. He really wants to be a good host.

Dani

In the last chapter, God tells Abraham that Sarah was going to have a son. Abraham fell down laughing. God pays no attention. God tells Abraham to name his son Isaac *meaning he laughs*. In this story, when three visitors come and repeat that Abraham and Sarah will have a son, Sarah laughs. God does pay attention when Sarah laughs.

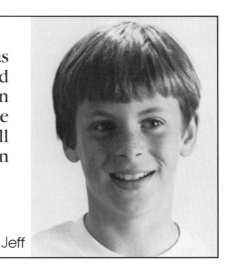

Jeff

At the end of the story, a big deal is made out of the fact that Sarah laughed. You could think that she laughed because she doubted God's promise. That would be bad. I think that God was proud of Sarah. It takes a lot of strength to laugh when someone is talking about the one thing that you have never been able to do. I think that Sarah really laughed with joy.

Sasha

SARAH LAUGHED—A CLOSE LOOK

SECRET MESSAGES

ACTION

In this story, 3 words are repeated. List these words and see what they teach you about ABRAHAM. Check your answer on page 214.

CONFUSION

Sometimes in a television show or a movie they show you two pictures at the same time. You see one picture over the other picture. Some places in this story are like that. Sometimes ABRAHAM and SARAH are seeing or talking to God. Sometimes they are hosting and talking to the visitors. Sometimes we are not sure. Divide the story into the parts where God is there and the parts where the visitors are there.

FIND WHAT CHANGED

SARAH said:

"Now that my time has passed,
how can my old husband and I have a child?"

God told ABRAHAM:

"Why is SARAH laughing and saying:
'Will I really give birth, now that I am old?'"

What did God change? Check your answer on page 214.

WHO SAID IT

At the end of this story, SARAH is told: **YOU DID SO LAUGH.**
The TORAH doesn't make clear who said this. Which of these do you think said it?

    a. ABRAHAM said it.
    b. GOD said it.
    c. One of the visitors said it.

CHAPTER 12

THE SODOM DEBATE Genesis 18.16-33

The men got up from there and looked down on SODOM.
ABRAHAM walked along with them.

The LORD said:
    "Should I hide what I am going to do from ABRAHAM.
    Since ABRAHAM is to become a great and numerous nation,
    and all the nations of the world
    will be blessed through him,
    I have become close to him
    so that he will command his children
    and his future-family.
    to keep the way of the LORD,
    to do what is **right** and just."

The LORD said:

"The shouting from SODOM and GOMORRAH is very loud.
And their sin is very heavy.
I will go down and I will see
if they are really doing as they are shouting."

The men turned from there and went towards SODOM,
while ABRAHAM stayed with the LORD.

ABRAHAM came close and said:

"Will you really sweep away
the **righteous** people with the guilty ones?
Maybe there are 50 **righteous** people in the city—
will you still sweep it away?
Won't you put up with the city
if there are 50 **righteous** people there?

You above all should not do this thing,
killing the **righteous** with the **wicked**.
as if the **righteous** and the **wicked** are the same.

Should not the Judge of all the earth
do what is just?"

The LORD said:

"If I find 50 **righteous** people inside the city,
I will put up with the city."

ABRAHAM answered:

"Please . . .
I dared to speak to my LORD
Even though I am only dust and ashes.
What if there are 5 less than
the 50 **righteous** people?
Will You destroy the whole city
because of 5?"

הֲשֹׁפֵט כָּל־הָאָרֶץ לֹא יַעֲשֶׂה מִשְׁפָּט

The LORD said:
    "I will not destroy it if I find 45 there."

But he continued.
    "Maybe only 40 will be found."

The LORD said:
    "I will not do it, because of the 40."

And he said:
    "Please don't be angry, my LORD, if I continue.
    Maybe only 30 will be found there."

The LORD said:
    "I will not do it if I find 30 there."

And he said:
    "Please . . .
    I dared speak to the LORD,
    maybe only 20 will be found there."

The LORD said:
    "I will not destroy it because of the 20."

And he said:
    "Please don't be angry, my LORD, if I continue
    one more time.
    Maybe only 10 will be found there."

The LORD said:
    "I will not destroy it, because of the 10."

The LORD left after speaking with ABRAHAM.
ABRAHAM returned to his place.

COMMENTARY

Abraham had lots of guts. I'm too scared to argue with a teacher or a principal. I do talk back to my mother sometimes but I don't think I could ever argue with God. God was great in this story. When I correct my mother she gets really angry—especially when I'm right. God really listened to Abraham.

Michael

God told Noah that the world was going to be destroyed and Noah didn't say anything. God told Abraham that two cities were going to be destroyed and Abraham started an argument. Abraham was great.

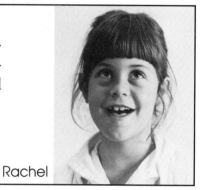

Rachel

World hunger, nuclear weapons, prejudice, cancer, and child abuse—these are things that people should stand up like Abraham and do something about.

Michael

I figure that this whole story was really a test. God already knew that there weren't 10 righteous people in Sodom and Gomorrah. God wanted Abraham to argue back. God wanted to teach Abraham that justice is worth arguing for. What I haven't figured out is why Abraham stopped at ten.

Laura

THE SODOM DEBATE—A CLOSE LOOK

SECRET MESSAGES

MAGIC SEVEN

Find the 'theme word' which is used seven times in this story. Check your answer on page 214.

MAGIC WORDS

כִּי יְדַעְתִּיו לְמַעַן אֲשֶׁר יְצַוֶּה אֶת־בָּנָיו וְאֶת־בֵּיתוֹ אַחֲרָיו וְשָׁמְרוּ דֶּרֶךְ יהוה לַעֲשׂוֹת צְדָקָה וּמִשְׁפָּט

**SO HE WILL COMMAND HIS FUTURE-FAMILY AND HIS HOUSEHOLD . . .
TO DO WHAT IS RIGHTEOUS AND JUST.**

In this story, God says that spending time with ABRAHAM was the best way of getting him to raise his children to be just and righteous. What do you think is the best way of raising children who do what is just and right?

הֲשֹׁפֵט כָּל־הָאָרֶץ לֹא יַעֲשֶׂה מִשְׁפָּט

SHOULDN'T THE JUDGE OF ALL THE EARTH DO WHAT IS JUST?

In the Talmud the Rabbis tell this story about Rabbi Meir: There were some robbers who were ripping off everyone in the neighborhood. After his home was broken into three or four times, Rabbi Meir got so angry that he prayed for the thieves to die. His wife Bruria scolded him. She said: "Don't pray for them to die, pray for them to stop sinning. If the wicked give up wicked ways, there will be no more evil." Rabbi Meir changed his prayer—he asked God to help the robbers change their evil ways.

Jews are supposed to **seek justice**. Where do you look for **justice**?

WORDPLAY

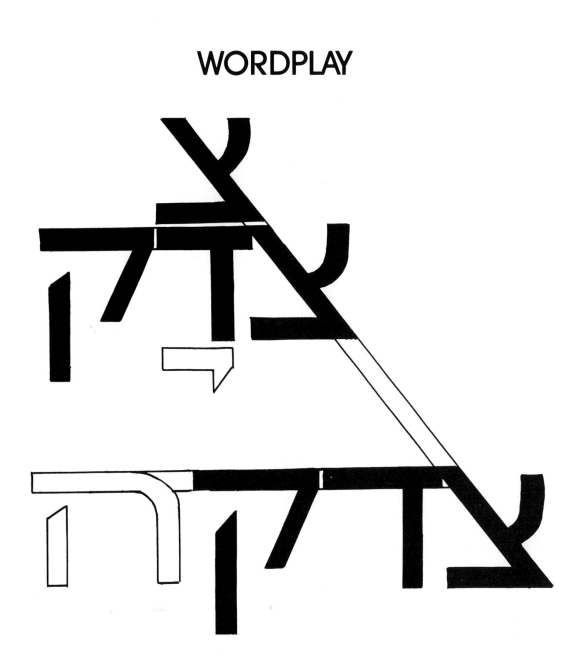

THE STORY OF A ROOT

Hebrew words are built out of roots. In this story, the root TZ*D*K is used seven times. Many Hebrew words are built with this root.

צֶדֶק TZEDEK—righteousness

צַדִּיק TZADIK—a righteous person

צְדָקָה TZEDAKAH—money shared to help others.

THE DESTRUCTION OF SODOM

The story of SODOM continues. Two visitors (angels) come to the city of SODOM. They meet LOT at the city gate. Like ABRAHAM, he invites them home as guests. That night the people of the town gather to hurt the two strangers, but LOT protects his guests. Before dawn, LOT's family sneaks out of the city with the angels. The angels warn the family not to look back.

God destroys the cities of SODOM and GOMORRAH. LOT's wife turns to look back and becomes a pillar of salt. ABRAHAM watches the destruction from far away. LOT and his daughters move to a cave in the hills.

VISITING ABIMELECH

ABRAHAM moves his camp to the Negev. There, King ABIMELECH of Gerar falls in love with SARAH. He doesn't know that she is married to ABRAHAM. When ABIMELECH finds out, he sends gifts to ABRAHAM to apologize.

CHAPTER 13

ISAAC IS BORN Genesis 21.1-8

The LORD **remembered** SARAH as the LORD **promised**.
The LORD **did** for SARAH as the LORD had **spoken**.

SARAH became pregnant and gave birth to a **son**.
ABRAHAM named his **son** ISAAC (meaning he laughs).
ABRAHAM circumcised ISAAC his **son**.
ABRAHAM was a **son** of 100 years
when Isaac his **son** was born to him.

SARAH said:
"God has made laughter for me.
Everyone who hears will laugh for me.
Who would have told ABRAHAM
that SARAH would nurse **sons**?
Well, I have given birth to a **son** for ABRAHAM's old age."

The boy grew
and ABRAHAM gave a party on the day
that ISAAC began eating solid food.

COMMENTARY

Abraham and Sarah take being parents really seriously. They are both proud. Abraham names and circumcises his son. Sarah makes a speech about how exciting it is to be a mother. Everyone in this story laughs for joy.

Amy

Stacey

Finally, God is beginning to make good on promises. Abraham and Sarah have been waiting long enough. At last, they are happy parents.

ISAAC IS BORN—A CLOSE LOOK

SECRET MESSAGES

THE CONNECTOR

The LORD **remembered** SARAH as the LORD **promised**.
The LORD **did** for SARAH as the LORD had **spoken**.

This story begins with these two sentences. Both of these sentences seem to be saying the same thing. Both are trying to remind us that God made a promise about SARAH. The fact that there are two sentences reminds us that this promise was made twice. Can you find both places God promises SARAH and ABRAHAM a son? Check your answer on page 214.

HAGAR AND ISHMAEL LEAVE

A little later, the story of ABRAHAM's other wife and other son continues.

SARAH asks ABRAHAM to have HAGAR and ISHMAEL leave the camp. ABRAHAM is upset, but God tells him to do what SARAH says. The next morning, HAGAR and ISHMAEL leave the camp and head into the wilderness.

Soon, they were out of drinking water. They are close to dying, when an angel appears, promises that God will make a great nation out of ISHMAEL, and leads them to water.

THE WATER WELL

ABRAHAM has a feud with ABIMELECH. Some of ABIMELECH's servants steal water wells belonging to ABRAHAM. ABRAHAM and ABIMELECH cut a covenant. ABRAHAM gets his wells back and the two groups live in peace.

CHAPTER 14

THE BINDING OF ISAAC

After these things
God tested ABRAHAM
and said to him:
"ABRAHAM."
He said "HINEINI" (meaning I am
here)
God said:
"Please—
take your **son**,
your only one,
the one you love,
ISAAC,
and **take yourself**
to the land of MORIAH
(meaning seeing)
and offer him as a sacrifice
upon one of the mountains
which I will tell to you."

וְהָאֱלֹהִים נִסָּה אֶת־אַבְרָהָם

ABRAHAM arose
early in the morning.
He saddled his ass.
He took two servants with him,
and his **son** ISAAC.
He chopped the wood
for the burnt sacrifice.
He went to the place
which God had told him.

וַיֹּאמֶר אֵלָיו אַבְרָהָם
וַיֹּאמֶר הִנֵּנִי

ISAAC spoke
to ABRAHAM his father.
He said: "My father."
He said: "HINEINI, my **son**."
He said: "HERE is the fire
and the wood,
but where is the lamb
for the sacrifice?"
ABRAHAM said:
"God sees a lamb
for the sacrifice,
my **son**."

The two of them
walked on together.

On the third day
ABRAHAM looked up and saw
the place in the distance.

ABRAHAM said to his servants,
"Stay here with the ass.
I and the lad—
we will go there,
we will worship,
and we will return to you."

ABRAHAM took the wood
for the sacrifice
and he put it on ISAAC his **son**.
He took in his hands
the fire and the knife.

The two of them
walked on together.

וַיֹּאמֶר יִצְחָק אֶל־אַבְרָהָם אָבִיו
וַיֹּאמֶר אָבִי
וַיֹּאמֶר הִנֶּנִּי בְנִי

An angel of the LORD
called to him from above:
"ABRAHAM—ABRAHAM."
He said: "HINEINI."
The answer came:
"Don't send out your hand
to the boy.
Don't do anything
to him at all,
because NOW I know
that you are in awe of God.
You didn't hold back your **son**
your only one,
from Me."

ABRAHAM looked up and saw.
HERE, behind him,
in the bushes,
a ram was caught by its horns.
ABRAHAM went.
He took the ram.
He offered it as a sacrifice
in place of his **son**.

They came to the place
of which God spoke.
ABRAHAM built the altar.
He spread out the wood.
He tied up ISAAC his **son**.
He placed him on the altar
on top of the wood.
ABRAHAM sent out his hand
to take the knife
to kill his **son**.

ABRAHAM called the name of that place:
ADONAI-YIREH (meaning the Lord sees).

The LORD'S angel called to ABRAHAM a second time:
"I myself promise—the LORD says,
'Because you did this for me
and did not hold back your **son**, your only one,
I will bless you by blessing you.
I will make you many, very many,
as the stars of the sky
and as the sand that is on the seashore.
Your future-family shall inherit the cities of their enemies.
All the nations of the earth
shall be blessed through your future-family.'"

ABRAHAM returned to his servants.
They got up and walked on together to Beer-sheba.

ABRAHAM made camp in Beer-sheba.

COMMENTARY

I hate this story. It really, really scares me. When I hear this story I get afraid that a father would kill his son—even if God told him to do it. I know my father loves me, but Abraham really loved Isaac. I know that it is important to believe in God, but no one should believe in God that much. This is not a good Jewish story.

Loren

They read this story on Rosh Hashanah. Last year, after the Torah service, my father and I had a long talk about it. He said that this story teaches us that sacrificing children is wrong. In Abraham's day, some nations sacrificed first born children to the local chief god. This story told everyone that there was one God and that God didn't want child sacrifice.

Wendy

This story confuses me. It starts out by having God test Abraham. Abraham is forced to make a choice between the God he loves and the son he loves. Abraham chose to follow God's orders. God stops him and gives him a blessing. Maybe God wanted him to argue back like he did with Sodom. I'm not sure he did the right thing.

James

THE BINDING OF ISAAC—A CLOSE LOOK

SECRET MESSAGES

A CONNECTING ECHO

This story begins with an order from God.

"Take your **son**, your only one, the one you love, ISAAC,
and **take yourself** to the land of MORIAH (meaning seeing)
and offer him as a sacrifice upon one of the mountains
which I will tell to you."

See if you can find a connection with the first order God gave ABRAHAM.

"Take yourself from your **land**, from your birthplace
from your father's house
to the **land**: there I will let you **see**."
Check your answer on page 214.

MAGIC NUMBERS

One word in this story is used 10 times. It is a **theme** word. Can you find it?
Check your answer on page 214.

Another important word in this story is the word **see**. Find the places it is used.
Check your answer on page 214.

MAGIC WORDS

HINEINI   הִנֵּנִי

HINEINI is an important word in this story. It means **I am here**. With this word, ABRAHAM answers the calls of God, his son, and the angel. It is also the way JOSEPH will answer his father, the way MOSES will answer God at the burning bush, and the way that Samuel will answer God's call in the Tabernacle. A famous Jewish commentator, RABBI SHLOMO BEN YITZCHAK (called RASHI for short), explains that HINEINI is the way a righteous person should answer. It says that you are ready and are paying your closest attention. It is like having a special HINEINI attitude.

Think of some times you should want to have the HINEINI attitude.

THEY WENT—THE TWO OF THEM TOGETHER וַיֵּלְכוּ שְׁנֵיהֶם יַחְדָּו

ISAAC trusted his father. He didn't understand the journey they took, but he followed his father's orders. To show us this the Torah says: **They went—the two of them together**. It says this twice. In a way, ISAAC passed the test, even as ABRAHAM did. Are there times to follow your parents orders, even when you don't fully understand the orders?

SARAH DIES

SARAH died at the age of 127. She died in the city of Hebron. ABRAHAM went to the elders of the city to ask for help buying land. They offered to help him.

He wanted help to buy the **Cave of Machpelah** from EPHRON. They bargained for a long time. Finally ABRAHAM bought the cave for 400 shekels. He buried SARAH in the cave. It was the first land that ABRAHAM ever owned.

REBEKAH: A SERVANT IS SENT

After SARAH died, ABRAHAM began to think about his own death. People do that. ABRAHAM calls for a servant and sends the servant back to the land of ABRAHAM'S birthplace to find a wife for ISAAC. This is the story of that servant's journey.

CHAPTER 15 **REBEKAH AT THE WELL** Genesis 24.10-20

The servant took 10 camels and some of his master's most precious things. He got up and went to the land of Aram between the two rivers.

He made the camels kneel down outside the city
by the water well.
It was evening,
the time when people go out to draw water.

He said:
"LORD, God of my master ABRAHAM
Please—may this be the day that you do
the **right-thing** for my master ABRAHAM.

I am standing here by the well
and the young women
are going out to draw water.
Let it be
that when I say to a woman
Please—may I drink from your jar?
one will answer,
Drink, and I will also draw water for your camels.
She will be the one that you have chosen for ISAAC.
And through this I will know
that You have done the **right thing** for my master."

וְעֲשֵׂה־חֶסֶד עִם אֲדֹנִי אַבְרָהָם

Almost before he could finish speaking
there came Rebekah, ABRAHAM's niece.
Her jar was on her shoulder.
She was very beautiful to look at.

The servant ran to meet her.
He said: "Please—let me drink a little water
from your jar."
She said: **"Drink, my master."**
She **hurried**.
She lowered her jar on her arm
and she let him drink.
When he had finished drinking, she said:
**"I will also draw water for your camels—
until they have finished drinking."**

Hurrying, she emptied her jar into the drinking trough.
Again she **ran** to the well to draw water.
She brought enough water for all the camels.

וַתְּמַהֵר וַתְּעַר כַּדָּהּ אֶל־הַשֹּׁקֶת וַתָּרָץ עוֹד אֶל־הַבְּאֵר
לִשְׁאֹב וַתִּשְׁאַב לְכָל־גְּמַלָּיו

COMMENTARY

After this story I'm sure that the Bible has lots of tests. Rebekah really passed this test. She definitely comes out a good, kind, nice person. She definitely won Miss Hospitality.

Brent

I wish we still had wells today. Wells seem to be a great place to make friends. I guess that's where people hung out before they invented malls.

Rachel

REBEKAH AT THE WELL—A CLOSE LOOK

SECRET MESSAGE

THE HIDDEN TEST

Here is the way the servant explains the test. Can you figure out what he was testing?

"Let it be
that when I say to a woman—
'Please—may I drink from your jar.'
One will answer—
'Drink, and I will also draw water for your camels.'
—let her be the one you have selected."

What kind of woman did it take to pass this test? Check your answer on page 215.

FIND THE CHANGE

Rebekah did more than just pass the test. How did she do more than the test required.

> **Drink, my master** . . .
> **I will also draw water for your camels—**
> **until they have finished drinking**

Check your answer on page 215.

SECRET WORD CONNECTIONS

Look at the way REBEKAH drew water. Look closely, and see if you can figure out how the words connect us to another story.

> She **hurried**. She lowered her jar on her arm
> and she let him drink . . . .
> **Hurrying**, she emptied her jar into the drinking trough.
> Again she **ran** to the well to draw water.

Check your answer on page 215.

MAGIC WORDS

DO THE RIGHT THING FOR MY LORD ABRAHAM וַעֲשֵׂה־חֶסֶד עִם אֲדֹנִי אַבְרָהָם

In this story the servant asks God: **"Please—do CHESED** (THE RIGHT THING) **for my master ABRAHAM."** CHESED means many things. It means kindness. It means mercy. It means faithfulness. When you do CHESED, you are doing more kindness or good than the law requires. Can you think of some acts of Chesed?

REBEKAH'S FAMILY

When REBEKAH finishes watering the camels, the servant gives her a gift of a gold ring for her nose and two golden bracelets. She tells him that she is NAHOR's granddaughter. NAHOR is ABRAHAM's brother. She invites the servant home to spend the night. He thanks God for doing the RIGHT THING for his master and for leading him to his master's family.

When he reaches her house, the servant is introduced to REBAKAH's brother LABAN. The servant tells LABAN the entire story. At the end of the story, the servant speaks to LABAN and BETHUEL, REBEKAH's mother. He asks permission to take REBEKAH to CANAAN, where she will become ISAAC's wife. The two of them answer:

> "This thing came from THE LORD.
> We are not able to say to you EVIL or GOOD.
> REBEKAH is before you.
> Take her and go.
> Let her become wife to your master's son.
> Just as the LORD has said."

At this point, the servant gives them gifts. They send for REBEKAH, and she answers: "I will go."

114

CHAPTER 16

REBEKAH MEETS ISAAC Genesis 24.59-67

They sent off REBEKAH.
They blessed REBEKAH:
"May you become **a thousand times many,**
and may **your future-family inherit**
the cities of their enemies."
REBEKAH and her maids got up.
They mounted the camels and followed the man.

ISAAC went out strolling in the field just before evening.
He lifted up his eyes and saw.
Camels were coming.
REBEKAH lifted up her eyes and saw ISAAC.

She got down off the camel.
She said to the servant:
"Who is that man walking towards us,
the one out there in the field ?"
The servant said: "He is my master."

ISAAC took her into his mother SARAH's tent.
He took REBEKAH to be his wife. He loved her.
ISAAC found comfort after his mother died.

COMMENTARY

I love it. The Bible believes in love at first sight!

Rochelle

REBEKAH MEETS ISAAC—A CLOSE LOOK

SECRET MESSAGE

A CONNECTION

When LABAN and BETHUEL bless REBEKAH, they give her two blessings: **May you become a thousand times many and may your future-family inherit the cities of the cities of their enemies.**

These words sound a lot like one of the blessings that God gave ABRAHAM. Find that blessing. Check your answer on page 215.

LOVE AT FIRST SIGHT

This story tells us that REBEKAH and ISAAC fell in love at first sight. Find the two sentences which show that they both saw each other and fell in love at the same time. Check your answer on page 215.

COMFORT

At the end of this story it says: **ISAAC took her into his mother SARAH's tent. He took REBEKAH to be his wife. He loved her. ISAAC found comfort after his mother died.** Look in the GARDEN story and find where the Torah explain the reason for marriage. It is very much like this story. Check your answer on page 215.

BIRTHS AND DEATHS

Before we continue with ISAAC's life-story, we have three quick stories whose texts we are skipping.

First: ABRAHAM took another wife and had a few sons. But he willed all that he owned to ISAAC.

Second: ABRAHAM died at the age of 175. Both of his sons, ISAAC and ISHMAEL buried him in the cave of the Machpelah near his wife SARAH.

Third: **This is the family history of Ishmael.** He had 12 sons and died at the age of 137.

Chapter 17 JACOB: ROUND 1—BIRTH, ROUND 2— BIRTHRIGHT Genesis 25: 19-34

This is the family history
of ISAAC, son of ABRAHAM.
ABRAHAM fathered ISAAC.
When ISAAC was 40 years old
he took REBEKAH as his wife.

ISAAC pleaded with the LORD
for his wife
because she had not
given birth to children.
The LORD let ISAAC's plea work,
and REBEKAH became pregnant.

Twins struggled in her womb,
and she said:
"If it is like this—
why am I living?"
She went to seek out the LORD.

The LORD said:
"Two nations
are in you.
The 2 families inside you
will be separated.
One nation shall be stronger
than the other.
The older will serve
the younger."

When it was her time
to give birth,
twins were in her stomach.
The first came out red.
He was hairy
like an animal skin,
so they called him ESAU
(meaning the hairy one).
After this
his **brother** came out,
his hand holding tightly
to ESAU's **heel**.
They called him JACOB
(meaning the heel-grabber).

The boys grew up.
ESAU became a man
who knew how to hunt,
a wanderer in the fields.

JACOB was a quiet man,
living in tents.

ISAAC loved ESAU
because he ate the meat from
the hunt.
REBEKAH loved JACOB.

JACOB was boiling stew
when ESAU came from the field.
ESAU was tired.
He said to JACOB:
"Please—let me gulp from the
red stuff—that red stuff."
Because of this, they called
his name EDOM
(meaning the Red-One).

JACOB said:
"First, sell me your
first-born right."

ESAU said: "I am about to die!
What good is the first-born
right to me?"

JACOB said: "Swear it to me
He swore and sold
his first-born-right to JACOB.

JACOB gave ESAU bread
and boiled beans.
He ate. He drank. He got up.
And he walked away.
This is how ESAU
wasted his first-born right.

WORDPLAY

In this story, we meet JACOB and ESAU.

In HEBREW, JACOB'S Name is יַעֲקֹב YA'AKOV. It is built around the the three letters ע ק ב which mean "heel." He is given the name YA'AKOV (meaning the heel-grabber) because when he was born he was grabbing ESAU's heel. It was like he was fighting to be born first. JACOB also plays lots of tricks. In English we could call a someone who plays a lot of tricks a **heel**.

ESAU has two names. At birth he was called עֵשָׂו **ESAV**, (which means the hairy one). He was born with a lot of red hair. Later on, ESAU's family will be known by a different name—**EDOM**. EDOM will be a large kingdom near Israel. **EDOM** אֱדוֹם , sounds like the Hebrew word אָדֹם **ADOM** which means red. It is built from the same word parts as דָם **DAM** (blood), אָדָם **ADAM** (the name of the first human), and אֲדָמָה **ADAMAH** (ground). The Torah says that the name comes from the red bean soup he bought from JACOB. Later on JACOB will also get a second name.

COMMENTARY

Scott

You know, I could imagine this chapter as a wrestling match. In this corner, the Big Red—the wild man from the fields—Esau, Isaac's favorite. In this corner, the kid from the tent, Jacob, Rebekah's favorite, with his famous heel grab. It even has the dirty tricks.

This story shows how important women are. God tells Rebekah what is happening and which son is going to be important. He doesn't do that for Isaac.

Amy

Josh

Once again we have a story of brothers fighting each other. I know that Jacob is going to come out the good and important brother, but in this story I just don't like him. He really is a sneak. It looks like we'll never get to a story where brother does keep brother.

If I had to pick between Jacob and Esau to be the future leader of the Jewish people, I'd look for a third choice. Jacob is a sneak. He doesn't do any work on his own. He just sits around camp stirring a pot. Esau is the hero type. He hunts and knows the woods and all that stuff. But he's so stupid that he actually forgets how important a first-born right is, and he sells it for beans. I mean, he really takes beans.

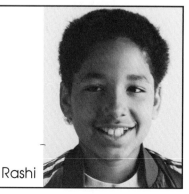

Rashi

121

JACOB: ROUND 1 AND 2—A CLOSE LOOK

SECRET MESSAGES

MAGIC NUMBERS

JACOB's name is used 10 times in this story (if you add the one time the word **heel** is used). ESAU's name is used 9 times and his other name EDOM is used once. This makes 10 too. Can we learn anything from this? Check your answer on page 215.

CONNECTION

ISAAC and REBEKAH had a problem that also happened to ABRAHAM and SARAH. What is this problem, and how does it make their children special? Check your answer on page 215.

PREDICT THE FUTURE

God tells REBEKAH: **"One nation shall be stronger than the other. The older will serve the younger."** In those days, the firstborn son was to inherit everything from his father. This means that ESAU should inherit both ISAAC's wealth and his special partnership with God. Based on this chapter, what do you think will happen?

MAGIC WORDS

IF IT IS LIKE THIS—WHY AM I LIVING?   אִם־כֵּן לָמָּה זֶּה אָנֹכִי

When the twins were fighting in her stomach, REBEKAH was in a lot of pain. It hurt so much that for that one moment she was sorry to be alive. If REBEKAH came to you crying, and she said: **"If it is like this—why am I living?"** What would you tell her?

A VISIT TO ABIMELECH

The Torah tells another story of a time when people were starving. This time God appears to ISAAC and says:

"Do not go to Egypt.
Stay in this land.
I will be with you.
I will bless you.
All these lands will be for you and your future-family.
I will keep the promise that I gave
to ABRAHAM your father.
I will make your future-family as many
as the stars of the sky.
All the nations will find blessing
through your future-family
All because ABRAHAM your father listened to My voice
and **kept** My mitzvot, My laws, and My Torah."

ABIMELECH, king of the Philistines, sees REBEKAH and falls in love with her. He takes her. When ABIMELECH learns that she is ISAAC's wife, he returns her. Then he commands his people to protect ISAAC's and REBEKAH's family.

A NON-WAR STORY

ISAAC plants and grows 100 times as much as he sowed. He grows rich, and ABIMELECH asks him to go because he now owns too much. He moves, but there is still a feud over who owns some wells. This happens several times over several wells. In the end, ISAAC and ABIMELECH make a covenant and let each other live in peace.

ESAU TAKES A WIFE

When ESAU is 40 he marries JUDITH and BASEMATH, 2 Hittite women. This makes both ISAAC and REBEKAH unhappy.

CHAPTER 18

JACOB: ROUND 3—THE BLESSING Genesis 27:1-40

When ISAAC was old
and his eyes were too weak to see,
he called his older son ESAU: "My son."
He said: "HINEINI/I am here."
He said: "I am old
and I do not know when I will die.
Please take your weapons, your arrows, and your bow,
and go out into the field and hunt me some meat.
Make me a tasty treat just like I love
and bring it to me and I will eat.
Then I can give you my **blessing**
before I die."

REBEKAH heard what ISAAC said to **ESAU his son**.
ESAU went out to the field to hunt game,
and REBEKAH said to **JACOB her son**:
"I heard your father speaking to ESAU your brother.
He said: 'Bring me meat and make me a tasty treat
and I will give you the LORD's **blessing** before I die.'"

Now, my son, LISTEN to my voice
and do what I command you.
Go to the herd and take two good kids.
I will make them into a tasty treat for your father,
just like he loves.
You will bring it to him.
He will eat.
And because of this he will **bless** you before he dies."

JACOB said to REBEKAH his mother:
"ESAU my brother is a hairy man and I am a smooth man.
Maybe my father will feel me,
and I will be a trickster in his eyes
and bring a curse upon myself, and not a **blessing**."

His mother said to him: "The curse will be on me, my son.
So LISTEN to my voice—go and get them for me."

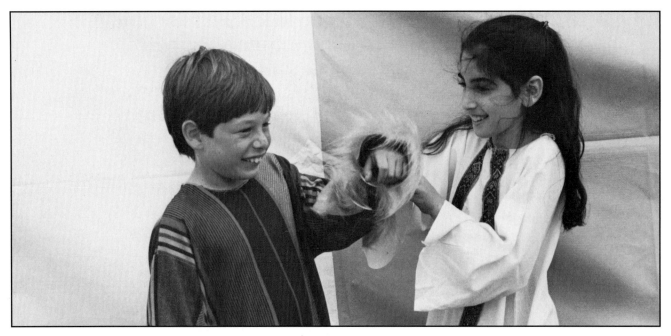

הַקֹּל קוֹל יַעֲקֹב וְהַיָּדַיִם יְדֵי עֵשָׂו

He went, he got them, and he brought them to his mother.
His mother made a tasty treat,
just like his father loved.

REBEKAH took her older son ESAU's clothes
which were with her at home,
and dressed JACOB, her younger son.
She clothed his hands and the hairless part of his neck
with the goats' skins.
She put the tasty treat and the bread she made
in her son JACOB's hands.

He came to his father and said: "My father."
He said: "HINEINI/I am here
Which one are you—my son?"

JACOB said to his father,
"I am ESAU your firstborn.
I have done what you told me.
Please—sit and eat my game
so that you can give me your **blessing**."

126

ISAAC said to his son:
"How is it that you found it so quickly, my son?"

He said: "The LORD your God made it happen for me."

ISAAC said to JACOB: "Come close to me and I will feel
you, my son, to find out if you are my son ESAU or not."
JACOB came close to ISAAC his father.
He felt him and said: "The voice is the voice of JACOB
but the hands are the hands of ESAU."
He didn't know him, because his hands were hairy
like his brother ESAU's hands.

He **blessed** him. He said: "You are my son ESAU."
He said: "I am."
He said: "Come close to me, I will eat
from my son's meat, so that I can give your **blessing**."

He came close to him. He ate.
He brought him wine. He drank.

ISAAC his father said to him:
"Please—come close and kiss me my son."

He came close and kissed him,
and he smelled the smell of his clothes, and **blessed** him.

"See, the smell of my son
is like the smell of a field which the LORD has blessed.

May God give you from the dew of the sky
and the richness of the earth
and much grain and new wine.
May nations serve you, and may peoples bow to you.
Be master over your brother,
and may the sons of your mother bow to you.
Let those who curse you be cursed.
Let those who **bless** you be **blessed**."

As soon as ISAAC finished **blessing** JACOB
JACOB left ISAAC his father
and ESAU his brother came in with his hunted meat.

He said to his father:
"Get up, my father, and eat from this hunted meat
so that you can give me your **blessing**."

ISAAC his father said to him: "Who are you?"
He said: "I am your son, your firstborn, ESAU."

ISAAC shivered.
He said: "Who was it who hunted meat, and brought it to me,
and I ate—before you came?
I **blessed** him and he shall stay **blessed**.".

When ESAU heard his father's words
he shouted a great and bitter shout.
He said to his father: "**Bless** me, too, my father."

He said:
"Your brother came, sneaked in, and took your **blessing**."

He said: "That is why he is named JACOB
(meaning the one who grabs heels).

He has grabbed from me two times.
The first time he took my birthright,
HERE, now, he took my **blessing**."

ISAAC answered ESAU:
"I have made him your master.
I gave him your brothers for servants,
I gave him corn and new wine.
What can I do for you, my son?"
ESAU said to his father: "Don't you have one **blessing** left for me?"
ISAAC his father answered him:
"You will live in the richness of the land.
The dew of the sky will be on it.
You will live by the sword and you will serve your brother.
But when you fight back, you will break free."

COMMENTARY

After this story I want to say the same thing as I said last story. Women are more important. Here Rebekah makes the right choice and sees to it that the right son is going to lead the Jewish people. If it was up to Isaac, we would have been stuck with a dumb hunter who marries a Canaanite women. I think Rebekah was a neat lady.

Amy

I don't think that Isaac was really fooled. I believe that he figured out that Jacob was pretending to be Esau, and decided to go along with it. It was the one way he could bless the son he wanted. Sometimes I even think (even though the Bible doesn't say so) that he might have set up the whole plan with Rebekah.

Brett

Jacob still looks like a sneak in this story. It is hard to think that one of the fathers of the Jewish people got there by sneaking and stealing a blessing. One thing about Jacob does makes me feel better. When Isaac asks him how he had hunted and cooked so quickly, he says: "The Lord your God made it happen for me." I don't think Esau would have ever mentioned God. This is one positive sign.

Peter

JACOB: ROUND 3—A CLOSE LOOK

SECRET MESSAGES

A MATCHING CLUE

In chapter 17, ROUND 1 and ROUND 2, the Torah tells us:
ISAAC loved ESAU because of the meat from the hunt. REBEKAH loved JACOB.
Can you find the matching clue at the beginning of this story? Check your answer on page 216.

FIND THE MISSING PART

Here is the blessing which ISAAC gave to JACOB.

> "May God give you from the dew of the sky
> and the richness of the earth
> and much grain and new wine.
> May nations serve you,
> and may peoples bow to you.
> Be master over your brother,
> and may the sons of your mother bow to you.
> Let those who curse you be cursed.
> Let those who **bless** you be **blessed**."

Here is the way that ISAAC told ESAU about that blessing:

ISAAC answered ESAU:

> "HERE, I have made him your master.
> I gave him your brothers for servants,
> I gave him corn and new wine"

Find the parts of the blessing ISAAC didn't repeat to ESAU. Check your answer on page 216.

A PREDICTION

In chapter 17, ROUND 1 and ROUND 2, we have two predictions about JACOB and ESAU. God tells Rebekah: **"One people shall be stronger than the other. The older will serve the younger."** How does this prediction start to come true in this story?

MAGIC WORDS

THE LORD YOUR GOD MADE IT HAPPEN   כִּי הִקְרָה יהוה אֱלֹהֶיךָ לְפָנָי

These are the words JACOB uses to explain to his father how he had hunted the meat so quickly. When you first think about it, it is a lie. When you think more about the prediction God made to REBEKAH, this explanation is true. How is this true? About what things could you say: THE LORD GOD MADE IT HAPPEN?

THE VOICE OF IS THE VOICE OF JACOB   הַקֹּל קוֹל יַעֲקֹב וְהַיָּדַיִם יְדֵי עֵשָׂו
BUT THE HANDS ARE THE HANDS OF ESAU

What did JACOB do with his voice? What did ESAU do with his hands? Which would you rather have, JACOB's voice or ESAU's hands?

TWO REASONS TO LEAVE

The Torah tells us about two different reasons why JACOB left home.

First, ESAU was angry about JACOB stealing both his first-born right and his blessing. He said: "After my father is dead, I will kill my brother JACOB." REBEKAH heard this and told JACOB. REBEKAH told JACOB to leave and to go to her brother LABAN.

Second, ISAAC and REBEKAH send JACOB off to look for a wife among REBEKAH's family.

CHAPTER 19

JACOB'S DREAM

JACOB went out from Beer-sheba and went towards Haran.
He came to a **place** and camped there when the sun had set.
He took one of the stones of the **place** and put it under his head.
He laid down in this **place**.
He dreamed.
HERE—a ladder was set up on earth.
Its top reached the sky.
HERE—**God**'s angels were going up and down on it.
HERE—**God** was before him and said:
"**I am the LORD God** of ABRAHAM your father and the **God** of ISAAC.
The land on which you are lying,
I will give it to you—and to your future-family.

Your future-family **will be like the dust of the earth.**
You will spread out
to the Sea,
and to the East,
and to the North,
and to the South.
All the families of the earth **will be blessed through**
your future-family.
I am with you.
I will keep you in all your goings
and I will return you to this soil
because **I will not leave you**
until **I have done all that I promised you."**

JACOB awoke.
He said: "For sure, **God** is in this **place**, and I didn't know it."
He was awestruck.
He said: "This **place** is awsome.
This is the house of **God**. This is the Gate to Heaven."

וְהִנֵּה מַלְאֲכֵי אֱלֹהִים עֹלִים וְיֹרְדִים בּוֹ

JACOB got up early in the morning.
He took the stone from under his head.
He set it up as a marker and poured oil on it.
He called the name of the **place** BETH-EL
(meaning the house of **God**)

JACOB made a promise.
"If **God** will be with me and keep me in this journey
on which I am going,
and if I am given bread to eat and clothes to wear,
and if I return in peace to my father's house,
then THE LORD will be **God** to me.

This stone which I put as a marker
will be the house of **God**.
I will tithe 10 percent
of everything given to me for You."

מַה־נּוֹרָא הַמָּקוֹם הַזֶּה

COMMENTARY

I've got to admit it. I always wanted to climb that ladder. It's kind of like Jack's bean stalk. You want to get to the top and you want to know what is there.

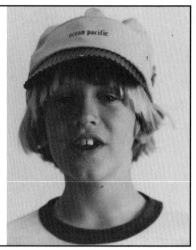

Randy

Ophira

I think that Jacob had guts. He had the courage to make a deal with God. None of the other Bible people ever did more than just listen to what God had to say. Abram waited almost his whole life for God's promises to come true. Jacob is different. He comes right out and says what he is thinking. He tells God, "I'm with You—if this all does come true." He had chutzpah.

This story is very important because it shows us that God was on Jacob's side. Up to now, Jacob stole or tricked people so that he could have what he wanted. In this story he doesn't do anything to force God's blessing. God blesses him because Jacob deserved to be blessed. Jacob deserved Isaac's blessing.

Shelly

JACOB'S DREAM—A CLOSE LOOK

SECRET MESSAGES

MAGIC NUMBERS

Count how many times the word God is used in this story.

Count how many things God tells JACOB.

(a) I am the LORD God . . .

(b) The land . . . I will give it to you

(c) Your future-family will be like the dust . . .

(d) You will spread out . . .

(e) All the families of the earth will be blessed . . .

(f)   I am with you.

(g) I will keep you.

(h) I will return you . . .

(i)   I will not leave you . . .

(j)   I have done all I promised.

What number does JACOB use in this story?

Check your answer on page 216.

FIND THE CONNECTION

When did God give another blessing which talks about North, South, East and West. Check your answer on page 216.

MAGIC WORDS

GOD IS IN THIS PLACE   יהוה בַּמָּקוֹם הַזֶּה

A mother told her daugher, "I'll give you a dollar if you tell me where God is?" The daughter answered her, "I'll give you 5 dollars if you tell me where God isn't."

While we know that God is supposed to be everywhere, it doesn't always feel that way. What are some of the places where you've felt close to God?

JACOB AT THE WELL

After JACOB makes his promise to God at BETH EL, the Torah goes straight to the story of his arrival at HARAN. He comes to a water well. This well is covered by a big rock that must be rolled off whenever it is to be used. It usually takes 2 or 3 people to move this rock.

At the well he meets RACHEL, who is LABAN's daughter. She is very beautiful. He rolls the big stone off the well all by himself. RACHEL brings him home. LABAN learns who JACOB is and says: "You are my bone and my flesh."

CHAPTER 20. **A DOUBLE WEDDING** Genesis 29.14-30

He stayed with them a month,
then LABAN said to JACOB:
"Just because you are like a brother to me,
why should you **serve** for me for free?
Tell me what payment you want."

LABAN had 2 daughters.
The older daughter was named LEAH.
The younger daughter was named RACHEL.
LEAH had weak eyes.
RACHEL was nicely shaped and nice to look at.
JACOB loved RACHEL.

He said: "I will **serve** for you for 7 years for RACHEL."
LABAN said: "It is better for me to give her to you
than to give her to any other man.
Live here with me."

JACOB **served** for RACHEL for 7 years.
In his eyes, it was just like a few days
because he loved her.

JACOB said to LABAN:
"Bring me my wife—for my days of labor are completed."
LABAN gathered all the people of the place.
He made a party with wine and food.
In the evening he took LEAH his daughter
and brought her to him.
(LABAN gave his woman-servant ZILPAH to LEAH
to be her maid.)

Morning came, and BEHOLD, there was LEAH.
He said to LABAN: "What is this you did to me?
I **served** you for RACHEL. Why did you trick me?"

LABAN said: "We don't do that in our place.
We don't give the younger daughter
before the older daughter.
Complete the wedding week
and I will give the younger to you, too,
as payment for **service** with me.
Serve for me another 7 years."

JACOB did this.
After the wedding week, LABAN gave him
RACHEL, his daughter, to be his wife.
(LABAN gave his servant BILHAH to RACHEL
to be her maid.)
JACOB married RACHEL and loved her more than LEAH.
He **served** another 7 years.

COMMENTARY

You, know Jacob and Rachel are a perfect team. He was the younger, and his father wanted his older brother to get everything. She was the younger, too, and even though she was the one who met Jacob, her father fixed it so her older sister marries Jacob. You just know that the two of them were made for each other.

Debbie

Laban is even trickier than tricky Jacob. He seems friendly and nice. He talks politely. Meanwhile, he is really sneaky. Maybe Jacob got what he deserved.

Tamir

If Rachel and Leah had a hard time sharing the same husband, the Torah doesn't tell us about it. Cain and Abel got into fights just by being brothers. Lot and Abram couldn't live together, just because of how much stuff they owned. Jacob and Esau fought over birthrights and blessings, but the Torah doesn't say a word about Rachel and Leah fighting. Each must have been good at being her sister's keeper.

Sabrina

A DOUBLE WEDDING—A CLOSE LOOK

SECRET MESSAGES

MAGIC NUMBERS

In this story, RACHEL's name is used 10 times and LEAH's name is used 7 times. Does this remind you of another story? Check your answer on page 216.

Count how many times the word **serve** is used. Check that answer, too.

TWO SENTENCES THAT DON'T BELONG

Two times in this story there are sentences that seem not to belong. Two times there are sentences that tell us something that Laban did for his daughters. These are clues to what will happen in the next story. Find these two sentences. Check your answer on page 216.

MAGIC WORDS

IT WAS JUST LIKE A FEW DAYS וַיִּהְיוּ בְעֵינָיו כְּיָמִים אֲחָדִים

At first, JACOB works for 7 years. The Torah tells us that it only felt like a few days because he was so in love with RACHEL. What are some long, hard jobs that felt short to you because you kept your goal in mind? What are some short jobs that seemed like they took forever? Why?

THE BATTLE OF THE BIRTHS

We are skipping 3 stories. In the first, 11 sons and 1 daughter are born to JACOB. LEAH and RACHEL have a kind of contest to see who can give birth to the most children. In the beginning, LEAH has four sons: REUBEN, SIMEON, LEVI, and JUDAH. RACHEL feels bad. Like SARAH and like REBEKAH, she can't seem to become pregnant. She does the same thing SARAH did for ABRAHAM. She gives JACOB her maid BILHAH as a secondary-wife. BILHAH becomes the mother of DAN and NAPHTALI. Not to be outdone, LEAH gives ZILPAH to be a secondary-wife to JACOB. She becomes the mother of GAD and ASHER. Then, once again, LEAH becomes pregnant and gives birth to ISSACHAR and then to ZEBULUN. Finally she gives birth to a daughter, DINAH. Then God remembers RACHEL. She becomes pregnant and gives birth to JOSEPH.

THE SPECKLED SHEEP

After JOSEPH is born, there is a second story. JACOB wants to leave LABAN and return home. The two of them make a deal. JACOB agrees to work for another season, and LABAN agrees to give him all the speckled and spotted animals in the flock. LABAN knows that there are very few speckled and spotted animals. Even so, LABAN sends all of the goats and sheep with markings to his son.

JACOB also plays a trick on LABAN. Somehow he makes sure that all the newborn kids and lambs are speckled or spotted. In this way, JACOB winds up a rich man.

LEAVING LABAN

JACOB gets in a fight with LABAN's sons. They say he stole from their father. He talks with RACHEL and LEAH. They tell him: "We won't be getting anything when our father dies. He sold us to you. Everything that God has allowed you to take from our father belongs to us and our children." When LABAN is away, JACOB and his family sneak out of town and head back to Canaan. LABAN catches up with them. JACOB and LABAN argue, but in the end they agree to separate.

CHAPTER 21

JACOB: ROUND 4—WRESTLING

1.

LABAN said to JACOB,
"LOOK at this small hill.
LOOK at this marker I planted between you and me.
I will not **cross** this hill toward you.
And you will not **cross** this hill and pass this marker toward
me to do evil."

LABAN arose early in the morning,
kissed his grandchildren and his daughters,
and blessed them.
LABAN left. He returned home.

2.

JACOB went on his way.
God's (messenger) **angels** met him.
When JACOB saw them, he said:
"This is God's camp."
He called the name of the place—MACHANIM.
(meaning two camps).

3.

JACOB sent **messengers** (angels) before him to ESAU his brother.
He commanded them, saying:
"This you shall say to my master, to ESAU.
'I have lived with LABAN.
I have cattle, asses, sheep, and servants.
I am letting you know this,
my master, to find favor in your eyes.'"

The **messengers** returned and said to JACOB:
"We came to your brother ESAU,
and he is on his way to meet you.
400 men are with him."
JACOB was very afraid.
He split his people and all that he owned into **two camps**.
He said: "If ESAU comes to one camp and attacks it,
perhaps the other camp will escape."

4.

JACOB said: "God of my father ABRAHAM
and God of my father ISAAC,
You said to me, 'Return to your land to your
birthplace and I will do **good** for you.'
I do not deserve Your mercy. I **crossed** the Jordan river,
and now my camp is split in 2.
Please save me from the **hand of my brother—
from the hand of ESAU**".

He camped that night.
He selected gifts from what was at **hand**
for his brother ESAU.
These he put in the **hand** of his servants.
He said to them: **cross** before me.
"When you see ESAU my brother, say,
'Your servant JACOB is sending presents to my master.
He is behind us.'"

JACOB thought:
"I will wipe anger from his **face**
by the gift that goes ahead of my **face**.
Later I will see his **face**,
when the gifts have **crossed** before his **face**.

וַיִּשְׁלַח יַעֲקֹב מַלְאָכִים לְפָנָיו
אֶל־עֵשָׂו אָחִיו

He awoke the same night.
He took his 2 wives and their 2 servants
and his 11 children
and **crossed** them **across** the Jabbok river.
He took them, and **crossed** them,
and had all that was his brought **across** the river.
And JACOB was left alone.
And a man wrestled with him until the dawn.
When the other saw that he could not win,
he touched JACOB's leg
and twisted his hip
while wrestling with him.
He said: "Let me go—the sun is rising."
He said: "I won't let you go unless you bless me."
He said: "What is your **name**?"
He said: "JACOB (meaning the one who grabs heels)."
He said: "JACOB is not your **name** anymore.
ISRAEL
(meaning the one who wrestles with God) is your **name**,
because you have struggled with God and with people,
and you can . . . ."

JACOB asked: "What is your **name**?"
He said: "Why do you ask my **name**?"
He blessed him there.

JACOB called the **name** of the place
PENIEL (meaning the **face** of God),
"because I have seen God **face** to **face**
and my life was saved."
The sun rose over him as he **crossed** PENIEL
(meaning the **face** of God).
He limped on his foot, because of his hip.

כִּי־רָאִיתִי אֱלֹהִים פָּנִים אֶל־פָּנִים

6.

JACOB looked up and saw ESAU coming with 400 men.
JACOB spread out his children
among LEAH, RACHEL, and the two maids.
He put the maids and their children first.
LEAH and her children were behind them,
and RACHEL and JOSEPH were at the back.
He **crossed** before them
and bowed to the ground 7 times,
until he came close to his brother.

ESAU ran to meet him.
He hugged him.
He kissed him and they cried.

ESAU lifted his eyes and saw the women and the children.
He said: "Who are these people with you?"
He said: "The children with whom the **LORD** has favored
your servant."

Then the maids and their children
came close and bowed.
Also LEAH and her children
came close and bowed.
Last, JOSEPH and RACHEL
came close and bowed.

And he said to him:
"Why did I meet your whole camp?"
He said:
"To find favor in my master's eyes."
ESAU said: "I have much, my brother.
Let what is yours be yours."

JACOB said: "Please, if I have found favor in your eyes—
take this gift from my **hand**,
because when I see your **face**,
it is like seeing the **face** of God.
You have been good to me.
Please take this gift-of-**blessing** that I brought you
because the LORD has favored me and I have everything."
He urged him and he took it.

ESAU said: "Let us travel, and I will go along with you."
He said to him: "Know that the children are young,
and the sheep and the oxen have newborns.
If you drive them hard the flocks will die.
My master, please—**cross** ahead of your servant,
and I will travel
at the speed of the herd and
at the speed of the children."

That day,
ESAU returned to Seir, and JACOB traveled to Succoth.
He built himself a house and made succoth for his cattle.
That is why the place is called Succoth.

COMMENTARY

I like what I discovered. The last thing that happened to Jacob when he left the land of Canaan was a dream about angels. Now, as soon as he comes back into the land of Canaan, the first people he meets are angels. The angels are like a border patrol for the land of Israel.

Adam

Jacob seems like a real wimp. I don't know why he is so scared of his brother Esau. He spends all his time sending gifts, calling Esau "my master," and trying to find favor in his eyes. He should have walked in bravely and said: "Listen, brother, I was a bratty kid, we've both grown up, I'm sorry I was such a brat."

Greg

Wrong! Jacob was smart. If he showed any muscle, Esau and his 400 men could have crushed him and his camp. By being polite and sending gifts Jacob forced Esau to be nice. It is no fun to be a bully if the other guy doesn't want to fight. Esau was stuck being nice to him.

Jennifer

This wrestling scene is another biblical story from the Twilight Zone. We don't know who Jacob is wrestling. It could be a man, or it could be an angel. It's really confusing. We talked about it a lot in class and Ilana Moskowitz came up with the idea that he was wrestling his fears. I had to think about that for a while. Now, I like her idea.

Ellen

You know, the Jacob in these stories is really a different person than the one who stole the blessing and the one who stole the birthright and the one who stole from Laban. The old Jacob thought only of himself. The new Jacob thinks about his family and his people. He tries to protect them and makes peace between his nation and Esau's nation. Jacob and Israel are almost totally different people.

Debbie

In class I asked a question no one could answer. The Bible says that the guy Jacob wrestled told him: "JACOB is not your name any more. ISRAEL is your name." He gets his name changed, but no one uses his new name. The story keeps on calling him Jacob and not Israel. That never happened after God changed Abram's name. My teacher says we'll find part of an answer in the next chapter, but I'm not sure.

Kenny

I know this sounds stupid, but I just figured out that the CHILDREN OF ISRAEL were really ISRAEL's children. When people said "THE CHILDREN OF ISRAEL," I always had this picture of Israeli kids running around. When we went over this story, I finally realized that Jacob's children become the 12 tribes. Jacob's name became Israel, so the CHILDREN OF ISRAEL really are ISRAEL's children.

Scott

ROUND 4: WRESTLING—A CLOSE LOOK

SECRET MESSAGES

MAGIC NUMBERS

The word **face** is used here 10 times.
The word **cross** is used 12 times.

Make a list of the things which are **crossed**, and see if you can figure out why this word is so important. Check your answer on page 217.

Make a list of the **faces** which are talked about and see what you can learn from this list. Check your answer on page 217.

THE CONNECTING "HAND"

When JACOB is thinking about meeting his brother ESAU (in part 3 of this story) there is one place where the Torah uses the word **hand** three times in a row. For some reason JACOB is thinking of ESAU's hands. Can you find out why? (CLUE: Look back at chapter 18, ROUND 3). In part 6 of this story, he tells ESAU, **"Please . . . take this offering from my hand."** Why are ESAU's hands important? Check your answer on page 217.

THE CONNECTING "NAME"

The name JACOB means the one who grabs heels. JACOB got this name because he was born holding his brother's leg. The name ISRAEL means one who wrestles with God. The "man" JACOB was wrestling gives him this name after pulling on JACOB's leg. How does this new name help JACOB/ISRAEL get ready to meet his brother?

THE CONNECTING "BLESSING"

When JACOB wins the wrestling match and the other person can't get free, JACOB asks for a **blessing**. JACOB already had the **blessing** that ISAAC gave him. Why do you think he wanted a new blessing? The "man" gives him a new name instead of a **blessing**. Why do you think that JACOB took this new name as his blessing? Check your answer on page 217.

TALKING BEHIND THE WORDS

The meeting between JACOB and ESAU is the first time they have seen each other since JACOB left home. JACOB left because ESAU was ready to kill him. When they talk to each other in this story, they are saying more than just the words they are speaking. Look at these sentences and see if you can explain the "feelings" that are being said with the words. Match the words they used with the feelings.

In the Bible		In their Minds
ESAU said:	"I have much, my brother. Let what is yours be yours."	Come on, we can be a family again.
JACOB said:	"Take this gift-of-blessing that I brought you."	Let me give you some gifts to make up for the blessing I stole.
JACOB said:	"The LORD has favored me and I have everything.".	I've done OK on my own, never mind what you stole from me. Besides I still have all the family possessions which you were supposed to get when you stole the first-born right.
ESAU said:	"Let us travel, and I will go along with you."	It's been good seeing you again, but you go your way and I'll go mine.
JACOB said:	"My master, please—cross ahead of your servant."	Don't worry that you kept all of father's possessions, God promised that I would come out on top and things are great.

MAGIC WORDS

I DON'T DESERVE YOUR MERCY

When JACOB leaves the land of Canaan to go to his mother's family, he asks God for help and protection. He makes a deal. He says: **"If God will be with me and keep me in this journey on which I am going, and if I am given bread to eat and clothes to wear, and if I return in peace to my father's house, then THE LORD will be God to me."**

This time, when JACOB asks for protection and help, he does it differently. He says: **"I do not deserve your mercy. I crossed the Jordan river, and now my camp is split in 2. Please save me from the hand of my brother from the hand of ESAU."**

Have you ever tried to make a deal with God? Have you asked God for something, even though you felt like you didn't deserve it?

BECAUSE YOU HAVE STRUGGLED WITH GOD AND WITH PEOPLE

The "man" who names JACOB says that JACOB has struggled both with people and with God. This is why he gives him the name "Israel." We know that JACOB struggled with ESAU and with Laban, they are people. How did he struggle with God? Have you ever "wrestled" with God?

DINAH IS ATTACKED

Next there is a story where DINAH, JACOB's only daughter, is attacked by Shechem, who came from the city of Shechem. In the end, JACOB's sons get revenge for the attack on their sister.

CHAPTER 22 **BIRTHS AND DEATHS** Genesis 35.1-26

God said to JACOB:
"Get up and go up to BETH EL (meaning the House of God) and settle there."

JACOB came to Luz, in the **land** of Canaan,
which is now BETH EL.
He built an altar there
and called the place BETH EL (meaning the House of God)
because there God came out of hiding to him
when he was escaping from his brother.

God appeared again to JACOB and blessed him:
"Your **name** is JACOB,
but no more will you be called JACOB.
Now ISRAEL will be your **name**."

God **named** him ISRAEL.

God said to him:
"I am God SHADDAI.
Be fruitful and become many.
A nation and a congregation of nations
will come from you.
The **land** which I gave to ABRAHAM and to ISAAC,
I give this **land** to you and to your future-family."
God went up from him—from the place where they spoke.

JACOB set up a marker in that place,
and he poured oil on it.
JACOB called the name of the place where God spoke to him
BETH EL (meaning the House of God)

They traveled from BETH EL,
but when there was still much **land**
between them and Ephrath,
RACHEL began to give birth. It was a hard labor.
As she was dying, she called his name:
"BEN-ONI" (meaning the son who gave me trouble),
but his father called him:
"BEN-JAMIN" (meaning my right-hand son).

RACHEL died, and was buried on the road to Ephrath
in Bethlehem.

JACOB now had 12 sons.
REUBEN, SIMEON, LEVI, JUDAH, ISSACHAR, ZEBULUN, JOSEPH,
BENJAMIN, DAN, NAPHTALI, GAD, and ASHER.

JACOB came to his father ISAAC in HEBRON.
This is where ABRAHAM and ISAAC stayed.
ISAAC was 180 years old when he died.
His sons ESAU and JACOB buried him.

COMMENTARY

When we talked about this chapter in class, Seymour said the story of Jacob pouring oil on the rock was just the Torah repeating itself. I thought he was wrong. It is like bookends. When Jacob left home and began his journey, he went to Beth El and met God. Now that his journey is complete he comes back to Beth El again, and again talks to God. Meeting God isn't a one-time thing.

Stacey

The funeral in this story is like the one when Abraham died. There, Isaac and Ishmael got back together to bury their father. Here, Esau and Jacob come back together to bury their father. Death seems to draw families closer together.

Michael

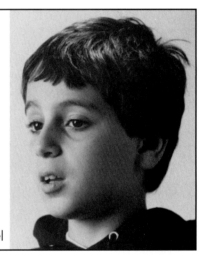

BIRTHS AND DEATHS—A CLOSE LOOK

SECRET MESSAGES

FIND THE CHANGE

This is the way the "man" changed JACOB's name.

> He said: "What is your **name**?
> He said: "JACOB (meaning the heel grabber)."
> He said: "JACOB is not your **name** anymore.
> ISRAEL (meaning the Godwrestler) is your **name**,
> because you have struggled with God and with people,
> and you . . . can"

This is the way God changed his name.

> "Your **name** is JACOB,
> But no more will you be called JACOB.
> Now, ISRAEL will be your **name**."
> God **named** him Israel.

What differences can you find? Check your answer on page 217.

AN ECHO

God also gives this blessing to JACOB: **"Be fruitful and become many"**. Where have we heard this blessing before? Check your answer on page 217.

A PROMISE COMES TRUE

As best you can remember, make a list of all the things that God promised to ABRAHAM, ISAAC, and JACOB. Which of these have come true so far? Check your answer on page 217.

CHAPTER 23

THE DREAMS COME TRUE

This is the family history of JACOB.

1.

JOSEPH (meaning the added one) was 17 years old.
He was a shepherd with his **brothers**.
JOSEPH made bad reports about them to his father.
ISRAEL loved JOSEPH best of all his sons.
He made him a robe of many colors.
When his **brothers** saw that his father
loved him more than all his **brothers**,
they hated him
and they could not speak peacefully to him.

וְיִשְׂרָאֵל אָהַב אֶת־יוֹסֵף מִכָּל־בָּנָיו כִּי־בֶן־זְקֻנִים הוּא לוֹ
וְעָשָׂה לוֹ כְּתֹנֶת פַּסִּים

JOSEPH **dreamed** a **dream**
and he told it to his **brothers**.
This added to their hate.

He said to them,
"Please, hear this **dream** which I **dreamed**.
We were tying bundles of grain out in the field,
when my bundle rose up
and your bundles gathered around and bowed to my bundle."
His **brothers** said to him:
"Are you going to be a king, being king to us?
Are you going to be a ruler, ruling over us?"
His **dreams** and his words added to their hate.

He said: "I **dreamed** another **dream**.
The sun, the moon, and 11 stars were bowing down to me."
When he told it to his father and his **brothers**,
his father scolded him:
"What kind of **dream** is this you **dreamed**?
Am I, your mother, and your brothers,
to come and **bow down to the ground** before you?"

COMMENTARY

Joseph was not a nice kid. He tells on his brothers. He brags about his dreams. He even makes his father feel bad. I don't think I would have liked him. But Jacob didn't start out as a nice kid, either.

Greg

This story is a lot like the Jacob story. We have a favorite kid. We have dreams, and we have a fight with brothers. Jacob was the one chosen to take over the future of the family. He became a better person when he grew up. Perhaps the same thing is going to happen to Joseph.

Stephanie

THE DREAMS COME TRUE—A CLOSE LOOK

SECRET MESSAGES

A MAGIC NUMBER

In all the stories we've read, we've seen a lot of places where the Torah says: **This is the family history** . . . . We have had the **family history** of The Heaven and the Earth, ADAM, NOAH, NOAH'S SONS, SHEM, TERAH, ISHAMEL, ISAAC, and ESAU. What should we notice about this **family history**? Check your answer on page 218.

AN ECHO

In this story, JOSEPH has two dreams. Both of these dreams predict that his family will bow down to him. One dream is about the earth. Here the crops that grow out of the soil bow down to JOSEPH. The second dream is about the sky. Here the sun, moon, and stars bow down to JOSEPH. Can you hear the echo of other stories in these two dreams? Check your answer on page 218.

ISRAEL said to JOSEPH:
"Your **brothers** are tending sheep in Shechem.
Come, I will send you to them."
He said to him: "HINEINI/I am here."
He said: "Please go
and check on your **brothers**
and check on the sheep.
Then return and tell me."

JOSEPH went after his **brothers**
and found them in Dothan.
They saw him coming.
Before he could get close,
they plotted against him
to kill him.

The **brothers** said to each other:
"HERE, the master of **dreams** is coming.
Let us kill him
and throw him in a pit,
and say a wild animal ate him.
Then we'll see if his **dreams** come true."

הִנֵּה בַּעַל הַחֲלֹמוֹת הַלָּזֶה בָּא

REUBEN heard this and tried to save him.
He said: "Let us not take his life."
REUBEN went on: "**Spill no blood**.
Throw him in this pit in the wilderness,
but don't lay a **hand** on him."
(This was so that he could save him
from their **hands** and return him to his father).

When JOSEPH came to his **brothers**
they stripped off his robe of many colors,
grabbed him, and threw him in the pit.
Then they sat down to eat bread.

וַיִּקָּחֻהוּ וַיַּשְׁלִכוּ אֹתוֹ הַבֹּרָה

COMMENTARY

Joseph looks like a nicer person in this part. He says "HINEINI" to his father and agrees to go to his brothers, even though that could be dangerous. He does know that his brothers hate him.

Shelly

Except for Reuben, Joseph's brothers were bad guys. Even if he did tell tales and brag a lot, he never hurt them. Here, just because of some dreams, they want to kill him. It is like they were afraid that his dreams would come true. The part that really bothers me is that they sat down and had a picnic right after throwing him in a pit. No feelings.

David

PART 2—A CLOSE LOOK

SECRET MESSAGES

REPEATED WORDS

The words **dream** and **brother** are both repeated.

Dreams are an important part of the story. In Bible times, people thought that dreams told the future. As we read this story, watch to see if these dreams come true, and watch for new dreams.

Here we have **brothers** who don't like each other. This reminds us of the stories of CAIN and ABEL and JACOB and ESAU. When the **brothers** want to kill JOSEPH, we think of the question: **Am I my brother's keeper?** One other sentence in this story connects it to the story of CAIN and ABEL. Can you find it? Check your answer on page 218.

3

They looked up and saw:
a caravan of ISHMAELITES were coming from Gilead.
Their camels were carrying gum, balm, and perfume
and they were going down to Egypt.

JUDAH said to his **brothers**:
"What do we get out of killing our **brother**?
Let's sell him to the ISHMAELITES
and our **hands** will not murder.
He is our **brother** and our flesh."

They grabbed JOSEPH,
pulled him up from the pit,
and sold him to the ISHMAELITES for 20 shekels of silver.
They brought JOSEPH to Egypt.

REUBEN came back to the pit.
JOSEPH was not in the pit.
REUBEN tore his robe.
He returned to his **brothers** and said:
"The boy is gone. What is going to happen to me?"

They butchered a goat
and dipped JOSEPH's robe in the blood.
They brought the robe of many colors
to their father and said:
"We found this.
Do you **recognize** it?
Is this your son's robe?"
He **recognized** it and said:
"My son's robe!
A wild beast has torn JOSEPH to pieces
and eaten him."

JACOB tore his robe
and mourned his son.

COMMENTARY

Two of Joseph's brothers try to help him. Judah and Reuben want to save Joseph, but they are afraid to speak out against their brothers. Sometimes I know what is right, but I don't say anything because I am afraid of what my friends will think.

Jon

I never told anyone this before. When I was little, my parents bought my baby brother a truck and I wanted one like it. They wouldn't buy me one. So once, when I got mad at my little brother, I broke his truck on purpose. I think that the brothers did the same thing with the coat. They wanted to kill Joseph, but they ruined his coat instead.

Matt

4

JOSEPH was taken down to Egypt.
POTIPHAR, PHARAOH's chief overseer,
bought him from the **hands** of the Ishmaelites.

The LORD was with JOSEPH.
He was a man who succeeded.
He lived in the house of his Egyptian master.
His master discovered that the LORD was with JOSEPH
when everything placed in JOSEPH's **hands** succeeded.
JOSEPH found favor in his eyes.

וַיְהִי יהוה אֶת־יוֹסֵף וַיְהִי אִישׁ מַצְלִיחַ

JOSEPH personally served him.
Everything that was his, he put in JOSEPH's **hands**.
The LORD blessed this Egyptian's house
because of JOSEPH.

JOSEPH was nicely shaped and nice to look at.

His master's wife **set her eyes** on JOSEPH
and said: "Love me."
He refused.
He said to his master's wife:
"My master has put everything in my **hands**
and he doesn't know what is happening in the house.
You are his wife.
How could I do such a great evil as this
and sin against God?"

She would ask JOSEPH every day,
and he paid no attention to her.

One such day, he came into the house to do his work.
No one else was at home.
She grabbed his robe, saying: "Love me."
He **left** his robe in her **hand** and ran away.

She called for the household slaves.
She said: "The Hebrew slave came to touch me.
When I raised my voice and screamed,
he left his robe and ran away."

When his master heard his wife's story,
he burned with anger.
He threw JOSEPH in the king's dungeon.

בַּאֲשֶׁר יהוה אִתּוֹ וַאֲשֶׁר־הוּא עֹשֶׂה יהוה מַצְלִיחַ

Even in the dungeon,
the LORD was with JOSEPH.
JOSEPH found favor in the eyes of the dungeon-master.

The dungeon-master put in JOSEPH's **hands**
all the prisoners
and all that was done there.
The dungeon-master didn't need to check on
anything JOSEPH did, because The LORD was with him.
Everything he did, the LORD made succeed.

COMMENTARY

Joseph seems to have a lot of luck, good and bad. If something can go wrong, it goes wrong for Joseph. No matter what, God turns the bad luck into good. Maybe this is one way to explain what the Torah means by "a man who succeeded."

Emily

My mother says that I have the same problem as Joseph. Joseph can't seem to hang onto a coat. First, his brothers take his coat of many colors and use it to show his father that a wild beast killed him. Now Potiphar's wife takes his coat and uses it to throw him in jail.

Michael

PART 4—A CLOSE LOOK

SECRET MESSAGES

GOOD THINGS HAPPEN TWICE

When JOSEPH was sold to POTIPHAR,

(1) The LORD was with him.
(2) Everything succeeded in his hands.
(3) JOSEPH found favor in his master's eyes.
(4) Everything was placed in his hands.

Find these same four things in the part of the story where JOSEPH is in the dungeon. What do you think the Torah is trying to teach? Check your answer on page 219.

THE HAND IS QUICKER THAN THE EYE

In this part of the story, both the word **hand** and the word **eye** are repeated.

The word **eyes** is the clue to the way three people look at JOSEPH. Name the three people. Check your answer on page 219.

The word **hand** is also a clue to a number of things. List the times that the word **hand** points to who owns JOSEPH. List the times that the word **hands** points to how JOSEPH takes over. And list the times that the word **hands** get JOSEPH in trouble.

A NICE CONNECTION

The Torah says: **JOSEPH was nicely shaped and nice to look at**. This is why Potiphar's wife wanted him. The Torah uses these same words about one other person. Can your remember who? Clue: Look in chapter 20. Check your answer on page 219.

MAGIC WORDS

THE LORD WAS WITH HIM   וַיְהִי יהוה אֶת־יוֹסֵף

When JACOB had to leave the land of Canaan, God told him: **"I will be with you."** This was one of the promises God made when JACOB dreamed of a ladder. Three times in this story, we are told, The LORD was with him. It shows us that JACOB's partnership with God passed on to JOSEPH. God is with the Jewish People. Are there times that you feel God is with you?

5.

PHARAOH, the King of Egypt, throws his BUTLER and his BAKER into the dungeon. The dungeon-master puts JOSEPH in charge of them. One night, both have dreams. The next morning they look sad. JOSEPH asks them what is wrong. They tell him:

"We **dreamed dreams**, and there is no one to tell us what they mean." JOSEPH said to them: "**Don't meanings come from God**? Tell me the dreams."

The BUTLER tells JOSEPH this dream: "I saw a grapevine with three branches. Before my eyes, the buds turned into flowers, and the grapes became ripe. I took the grapes and made wine for PHARAOH's cup. Then I gave the cup to PHARAOH." JOSEPH explains: "In three days, PHARAOH will bring you back to be his BUTLER again."

JOSEPH says to him:
At the right time, remember me.
Please, do **what is right** by me.
Remind PHARAOH about me, and take me out of this dungeon.
I was stolen from the land of the Hebrews,
and here I am innocent,
yet they put me in this pit.

Next the BAKER tells his dream: "I had three baskets on my head. In the top basket were baked goods for PHARAOH. Birds came and ate from the basket." JOSEPH explained: "In three days, PHARAOH will have you killed."

Three days later, is PHARAOH's birthday. He has the BUTLER return to his job, and the BAKER, he has killed. The dreams come true, just as JOSEPH explained.

But the BUTLER forgot about JOSEPH.

6.

Two years later, PHARAOH has a dream. He dreams about standing by the Nile and and seeing seven fat cows come out to graze. Next, seven skinny cows come out eat and the fat cows. PHARAOH wakes up.

When he falls back to sleep, he has a second dream. Seven good ears of grain are growing on one stalk. Behind them are seven thin and dry ears of grain. The seven thin ears eat the good ears.

No one can explain PHARAOH's dreams. Not even his magicians and not even his wise men know what they mean. The BUTLER suddenly remembers JOSEPH, who knows the meaning of dreams. He tells PHARAOH about JOSEPH.

SOME THINGS TO THINK ABOUT

1. JOSEPH had two dreams which seemed very much the same. Then the BUTLER and the BAKER have two dreams which come true. Now PHARAOH has two dreams which seem the same (and which will come true).

2. When JOSEPH tells his story, he calls the dungeon a pit. Two times he has been thrown down into a **pit** even though he was innocent.

3. JOSEPH says that God makes the meaning of dreams. JOSEPH also told Potiphar's wife that he would not sin before God.

4. When we hear JOSEPH's story about the way he came to be in the dungeon, it also sounds like the way the Jews will becomes slaves in Egypt.

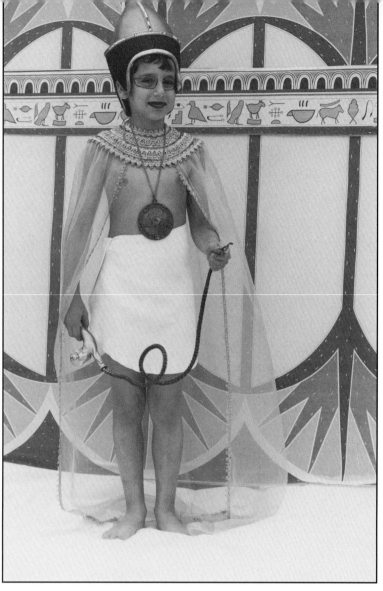

7.

PHARAOH sent for JOSEPH. They hurried him from the pit.
His hair was cut. His clothing was changed.
He was brought to PHARAOH.

PHARAOH said to JOSEPH: "**I have dreamed a dream,**
and there is no one to tell me what it means.
I have heard about you.
It is said that you know the meanings of **dreams.**"
JOSEPH answered PHARAOH: "Not I.
God will answer for PHARAOH's peace."

בִּלְעָדָי אֱלֹהִים יַעֲנֶה אֶת־שְׁלוֹם פַּרְעֹה

JOSEPH said to PHARAOH:
"PHARAOH's dreams, they are one.
God has told PHARAOH what will happen.
The 7 good cows are 7 years.
The 7 good ears of grain are 7 years.
They are one **dream**.
The 7 skinny cows that followed are 7 years.
The 7 thin ears of grain are 7 years of famine.

What I have told PHARAOH
is what God has shown you will happen.
7 years of plenty are coming to the land of Egypt.
And they will be followed by 7 years of famine.
PHARAOH had two **dreams** because this thing is true.
It came from God, and God will quickly do it.

NOW, let PHARAOH pick a true and wise person
and put him in charge of the land of Egypt.
Let PHARAOH appoint managers over the land
during the 7 years of plenty.
Collect all kinds of food from the good years to come
and store it and keep it.
This food will be for the 7 bad years which will come.
No one in the land of Egypt will die from the famine."

The plan was good in PHARAOH's eyes.

PHARAOH said:
"How could we find another person like this
who has the spirit of God in him?"

PHARAOH said to JOSEPH:
"Since God made all this known to you,
no one could be
as true and as wise as you.
You will be over my house.
You will command my people.
Only because of my throne will I be greater than you.
See, I give you all the land of Egypt."

PHARAOH took the signet ring off his **hand**
and put it on JOSEPH's.
He dressed him in robes of fine linen
and placed a gold chain around his neck.

COMMENTARY

Brett

Once again Joseph's bad luck turns into good luck. This time I think he deserves it. Even though I didn't like him at the beginning of the story, when he told tales about his brothers and bragged about his dreams, I like him now. You know, it looks like those dreams are going to come true. What I really like is the fact that he gives God credit for everything.

Joseph does a lot more than tell what dreams mean. He also teaches Pharaoh how to be a good king. Joseph's plan teaches Pharaoh to care for and protect all the people of Egypt.

Phillip

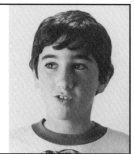

PART 7—A CLOSE LOOK

SECRET MESSAGES

THE RULE ABOUT 2 DREAMS

PHARAOH had 2 dreams which seemed the same. JOSEPH gave the meaning of those dreams to PHAROAH. JOSEPH also had 2 dreams (back in part 1) which seemed the same. What did JOSEPH teach PHARAOH about the meaning of having 2 dreams. Does that teach us something new about JOSEPH's 2 dreams? Check your answer on page 219.

REPEATED SENTENCE

PHARAOH says: **"I have dreamed a dream and there is no one to tell me what it means."** Where have we heard these words before? Check your answer on page 219.

HAND, EYES, and CLOTHES

In this JOSEPH story, we have been able to use the words **hands** and **eyes** to follow the ups and downs in JOSEPH's life. What do they teach us in this part? In the JOSEPH story, his clothes have gotten him in trouble twice. What do his new clothes do in this part of the story? Check your answer on page 219.

8.

The people of Egypt follow JOSEPH's plan. They store food during the 7 good years. Then the bad years come. Meanwhile, JOSEPH marries and has two sons named MANASSEH and EPHRAIM. The years of hunger come.

9.

The famine was everywhere
JOSEPH opened all the storehouses
and gave shares of grain to the Egyptians.
There was great hunger in Egypt.
From all the earth, people came to Egypt
to get food from JOSEPH.
There was great hunger everywhere.

10 of JOSEPH's **brothers** went down to Egypt
to get food.
But JACOB didn't send BENJAMIN,
saying, "Something might happen to harm him."
The children of Israel were among those
who came to Egypt because of the famine
in the land of Canaan.

JOSEPH's **brothers** came
and **bowed to the ground before him**.
When JOSEPH saw his **brothers**,
he **recognized** them
but treated them as strangers.
He spoke to them harshly:
"Where did you come from?"
They said: "From the land of Canaan, to get food."
JOSEPH remembered the **dream** which he **dreamed**.

COMMENTARY

Joseph's dreams really did come true. In the end, his brothers did bow down to him. But it isn't a bad thing. I think Joseph didn't tell his brothers who he really was because he wanted to test them. He had changed over the years, and he wanted to see if they had changed, too.

Mara

Joseph was a really good Jew. Not only did he make sure that everyone in Egypt had food, but he fixed it so that Egypt fed even strangers who asked for food. Joseph didn't let anyone go hungry. That is the Jewish way.

Sam

10.

JOSEPH says to his brothers, "You are spies." They deny it. To prove that they are not spies, they tell him the story of the whole family. They say, "We are 12 sons of one man, but the youngest son is still with his father, and the other one is no more." He wants to test them. He asks them to bring the youngest son down to Egypt. He has them locked up for 3 days. There the brothers talk. One says: "This is happening as punishment for what we did to JOSEPH." REUBEN says: "I told you not to harm the boy." JOSEPH heard this and could understand them, even though they thought he couldn't speak their language. JOSEPH goes and cries.

At the end of the three days JOSEPH gives them bags of grain, but hides their money in the bags. He sends 9 of them back to his father and keeps SIMEON in Egypt, to make sure that they will return.

11.

The famine is still bad. Even though they don't want to go back to Egypt, the brothers have no choice. JUDAH talks JACOB into letting them take BENJAMIN back with them. When JOSEPH sees BENJAMIN, he invites the brothers to eat dinner with him. They are afraid because of the money that was returned, but JOSEPH's servant explains:

> "Be at peace. Don't be afraid.
> Your God and the God of your fathers
> gave you a treasure in your sacks."

First SIMEON comes in and then JOSEPH. The brothers bow to the ground before him a second time. When JOSEPH meets BENJAMIN he cries, but he hides his tears from his brothers. He washes his face and the food is served.

Once again he sends the brothers back to Canaan with bags of grain. This time he hides a silver cup in BENJAMIN's bag. At the border the brothers are stopped, the silver cup is discovered, and they are brought back before JOSEPH.

12

JUDAH came close to him:
"My master,
please
let your **servant** (JUDAH) speak to you.
Don't get angry at your **servant** (JUDAH),
because you are like PHARAOH to him.

Now if I come to your **servant** (my father),
and the boy is not with us,
he will die.
Your **servant** (JUDAH) pledged to my father about the boy,
If I do not bring him back,
I will have sinned before my father."
NOW,
please
let your **servant** (JUDAH) be a **slave** to you instead of the boy.
LET the boy go up with his **brothers**."

כִּי לְמִחְיָה שְׁלָחַנִי אֱלֹהִים לִפְנֵיכֶם

JOSEPH couldn't control himself.
He ordered: "Everyone leave me."
When no one else was there,
JOSEPH **made himself known** to his brothers.
He lifted his voice and cried.
Egypt heard him. PHARAOH's house heard him.

JOSEPH said to his **brothers**: "I am JOSEPH, is my father still alive?"
His brothers were too surprised to answer.
JOSEPH said: "Please, come close to me."
They came close, and he said: "I am JOSEPH your **brother**,
the one you sold into Egypt.
NOW, do not be pained. Do not feel guilty that you sold me.
God sent me before you to save life.

Hurry, go up to my father and say to him:
'God put JOSEPH your son as master over all Egypt.
Come down to me. Settle in the land of Goshen and be near me.'"

COMMENTARY

I like happy endings. Joseph followed God's plan. He saved the family. He fed the world. He even taught his brothers a lesson and helped them to be better people. He used all his power to help people. He was even free enough to cry.

Loren

I don't think that Joseph should have played games with his brothers. I think he used his power to get even, and that wasn't right. Even though everything worked out for the best, I don't think he should have scared his brothers and made his father worry.

Ellen

Chapter 24

THE NEW KING

These are the names of the children of ISRAEL
who came to Egypt with JACOB.
Each man came with a household:
REUBEN, SIMEON, LEVI, and JUDAH.
ISSACHAR, ZEBULUN, and BENJAMIN.
DAN and NAPHTALI, GAD and ASHER.
JACOB's family grew to 70 people.
JOSEPH was already in Egypt.

JOSEPH died along with his brothers
and all the people of that generation.
The children of Israel were **fruitful**.
They **increased**.
They **became many**.
They **became very very strong**.
They **filled the land**.

There rose a new king over Egypt.
He said to his people:
"HERE, the **nation** of the Children of Israel
are many and stronger than we.
Let's outsmart them,
because if there is a war they might join our enemies
and fight against us and leave this land."

They put taskmasters over them to make
them suffer while they worked.
The Children of Israel built the cities of Pithom and Raamses.
THE MORE THEY MADE THEM SUFFER, THE MORE THEY MULTIPLIED
and the more they spread out.
The Egyptians were afraid of the Children of Israel.
The Egyptians made SLAVES of the Children of Israel.
They made their life bitter with hard SLAVERY—
SLAVING with cement and bricks and in the fields.

The King of Egypt spoke to the Hebrew's midwives.
They were named SHIPHRAH and PUAH.
He said: "When you help the Hebrew women deliver a baby
and you see that it is a boy, kill it. If it is a girl, she may live."

The midwives were in awe of God
and did not do what the King of Egypt told them to do.
The King of Egypt called for the midwives.
He said to them: "Why did you let the children live?"
The midwives said to Pharaoh: "Hebrew women aren't like
Egyptian women. They have easy deliveries and sometimes
their children are born before the midwife arrives."

God made it GOOD for the midwives.
Because the midwives were in awe of God,
God made them the mothers of great families.

Pharaoh commanded his whole people:
"Every Hebrew son which is born you will throw into the river.
The daughters can live."

COMMENTARY

This story is totally different from any before it. Up to now, we've been reading the story of a family. Now we have a nation. God promised Abraham and everyone that his family would become a nation. It did. It happened really fast.

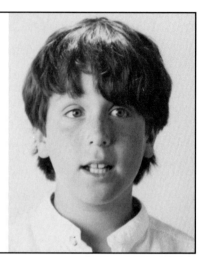

Jeff

This Pharaoh was crazy. He had nothing to be afraid of. He started hurting the Jews because he was afraid of something they might do. They hadn't done anything to bother anyone. It's like he hated them for no reason. That doesn't make any sense.

Sasha

When I read this story, I didn't know what a midwife was. My father explained that a midwife was sort of like a nurse except that she only helped women deliver babies. The midwives were really brave to stand up to a king and refuse to follow his orders. Not everyone has the courage to refuse to obey an evil order.

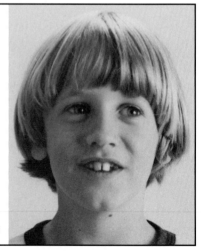

Randy

THE NEW KING—A CLOSE LOOK

SECRET MESSAGES

MAGIC NUMBERS

Count how many different ways the Torah tells us that Israel's family was growing. Then count how many different things PHARAOH tried to do to stop them from growing. Then read this sentence from the story: **The more they made them suffer, the more they multiplied.** Putting these all together, what can you learn? Check your answer on page 219.

Find the word that is used seven times in this story. Check your answer on page 219.

A PREDICTION COMES TRUE

God gave this warning to ABRAHAM. Find the place where God made this prediction. Read it again to discover what must happen next. Check your answer on page 219.

Back in chapter 9, A COVENANT,

> The LORD said to ABRAM: "Know for a fact
> that your future-family will be strangers
> in a land which is not theirs.
> They shall be slaves and suffer for 400 years.
> But I will punish the nation they serve,
> and after that, they will exit with riches."

MAGIC WORDS

GOD MADE IT GOOD FOR THE MIDWIVES וַיֵּיטֶב אֱלֹהִים לַמְיַלְּדוֹת

One Torah idea is that God does good things for people who do good. Sometimes the Torah points this out. Do you think that good things always happen to people who do good? (Check the stories of SARAH and JOSEPH)

Chapter 25

AND INTRODUCING MOSES Exodus 2.1-25

1.

A man from the tribe of Levi
married a **daughter** of the tribe of Levi.
The woman became pregnant and gave birth to a son.
She saw that he was GOOD.
She hid him for 3 months.
When she was no longer able to hide him,
she took an ARK of bulrushes,
covered it with slime and tar, put him in it,
and put it in the reeds on the bank of the Nile.
His sister watched from a distance
to know what would happen to him.

Pharaoh's **daughter** came down to the NILE to bathe.
She saw the ark in the reeds and
sent her servant to get it.
She opened it and saw a child,
a boy, crying.
She felt pity for him.
She said: "This is a Hebrew child."

Then his sister said to Pharaoh's **daughter**:
"Shall I go and call a Hebrew woman
to nurse the child for you?"
Pharaoh's **daughter** said to her: "Go."
She went and called the child's mother.

Pharaoh's **daughter** said to the mother:
"Go and take this child.
Nurse him and I will pay you."
The woman took the child and nursed him.

The child grew up.
The mother took him to Pharaoh's **daughter**.
He became her son.
She named him MOSES, saying:
"MOSES means I drew him from the water."

2.

When MOSES grew up
he went out to his brothers.
He saw their suffering.
He saw an Egyptian man beating a Hebrew man—
one of his brothers.
He looked this way and that way.
No one was around.
He killed the Egyptian and hid him in the sand.

He went out the next day.
Two Hebrew men were fighting.
He said to the guilty one:
"Why are you beating your neighbor?"
He said: "Who made you our boss and our judge?
Do you want to kill me, too,
just like you killed the Egyptian?"
MOSES was afraid—he said: "The thing is known."

When Pharaoh learned of this, he wanted to kill MOSES.

3.

MOSES escaped.
He came to settle
in the land of Midian.

He sat by a well.
The priest of Midian
had 7 **daughters**.
They came and drew water
for their father's sheep.

Some shepherds came
and drove them away.
MOSES stood up and saved them.
He gave water to their sheep.

When they came to their father,
he said: "How did you manage to
come home so quickly today?"
They said to him: "An Egyptian
man saved us from the hand of
the shepherds. He also drew
water many times for us, and
gave water to the sheep."

He said to his **daughters**:
"Where is this man?
How could you leave him?
Call him and he will eat with us."
MOSES was happy
to stay with the man.
One **daughter**, ZIPPORAH,
became MOSES' wife.
She gave birth to a son.
He named his son GERSHOM
(meaning the stranger).
He said: "I have been
a **stranger** in a **strange** land."

גֵּר הָיִיתִי בְּאֶרֶץ נָכְרִיָּה

COMMENTARY

Let me tell you a story. A man and a woman have a baby whose life is in danger. To save his life, they pack him up and send him away. Someone else finds him and raises him. Because he is different from everyone else, he grows up to be a great leader and help lots of people. Do you know this story? (Look at the bottom).

Josh

Moses must have been a good Jew from the start. Even though he was raised in Pharaoh's palace, he thinks of the Children of Israel as his brothers. When he sees one brother in trouble, he tries to be a good "keeper" and help him.

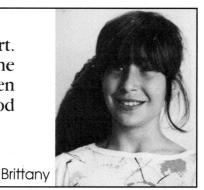

Brittany

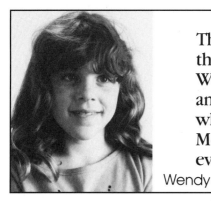

There is a great lesson in this story. We shouldn't think of all people from one nation as being the same. We sometimes think of the Egyptians as being bad and cruel, yet it is Pharaoh's daughter, an Egyptian, who saves the Jewish people. She even knows that Moses is a Jew from the start. This teaches us that every nation has good people.

Wendy

Here is the answer. I know that you thought that this is the story of Moses. Well, it isn't. It is the story of *Superman*. In some ways Moses and Superman are very much alike. One was a "strange visitor from another planet," the other was "a stranger in a strange land."

Josh

AND INTRODUCING MOSES — A CLOSE LOOK

SECRET MESSAGES

REPEATED WORD

This chapter tells three stories. These stories are all connected by one word. Find that word.

Check your answer on page 220.

ECHOES

Most pictures of MOSES in the bulrushes show MOSES floating in a basket. The Torah uses the Hebrew word תֵּבָה teva for the "basket." There is only one other place in the Torah where something is called a **teva**—in the story of NOAH—teva is the "ark." Why do you think that Torah wanted to compare NOAH and MOSES? How are they a like? Check your answer on page 220.

There is a second echo in this story. When MOSES is born, the Torah tells us: **The woman become pregnant and gave birth to a son. She saw that he was GOOD.** In chapter 1, BEGINNINGS, when God looks at things God created, **God sees that it is GOOD.** Why do you think that the Torah wants us to compare the creation of the world and the birth of MOSES? Check your answer on page 220.

BROTHERS KEEPER

In this story, MOSES is raised in PHARAOH's palace. The Torah tells us **he went out to his brothers**. When he gets there, he sees an Egyptian hurting a Jew. He helps the Jew. What does the word **brother** teach us about MOSES in this story?

MAGIC WORDS

I AM A STRANGER IN A STRANGE LAND גֵּר הָיִיתִי בְּאֶרֶץ נָכְרִיָּה

God told ABRAHAM that his future-family would be **strangers** in a land that was not theirs. Now this is coming true. In this story, MOSES has to run from EGYPT and becomes a **stranger** in another land. Later in the Torah God will teach the Children of Israel to remember that they were **strangers**. Why is it important to know how strangers feel?

THE BURNING BUSH

Exodus 2.23-3.

The King of Egypt died.
The Children of Israel
were groaning from slaving.
They cried out, and their cry
came up to God.

God **heard** them.
God **remembered** the covenant
with ABRAHAM,
with ISAAC,
and with JACOB.
God **saw** the Children of Israel.
God **knew**.

MOSES was tending his
father-in-law JETHRO's sheep.
He led the sheep
into the wilderness and came
to Horeb, the Mountain of God.
An angel of God **appeared** to him
in the flame of a burning bush.
He **saw**—and HERE—
the bush was burning
but not burnt by the flames.
MOSES said: "I must turn aside
to **see** this wonderful **sight**.
Why isn't the bush burnt?"
God **saw** that he turned aside.
God called to him
from the bush:"MOSES, MOSES."
He said: "HINEINI/I am here."
God said: "Don't come close.
First, take off your sandals.
This place where you are
standing is holy ground.

וַיִּשְׁמַע אֱלֹהִים
אֶת־נַאֲקָתָם
וַיִּזְכֹּר אֱלֹהִים
אֶת־בְּרִיתוֹ
אֶת־אַבְרָהָם
אֶת־יִצְחָק
וְאֶת־יַעֲקֹב
וַיַּרְא אֱלֹהִים
אֶת־בְּנֵי יִשְׂרָאֵל
וַיֵּדַע אֱלֹהִים

I am the God of your fathers,
the God of ABRAHAM,
the God of ISAAC, and
the God of JACOB."
MOSES hid his face because he
was afraid to look at God.

The LORD said:
"I have **seen** and **seen** again
the suffering of My people in Egypt.
I have **heard** their cry—
I **know** their pain.
I have come down to save them
from the hands of the Egyptians
and to bring them up
to land both good and wide,
to a land of milk and honey,
to Canaan.

Now I am sending you to Pharaoh,
and you will bring My people,
The Children of Israel,
out from Egypt."
MOSES said:
"Who am I, that I should
go to Pharaoh?
Who am I that I should
bring out the Children of Israel?"

God said: "**I will be with you**.
Let this be a sign for you,
for I have sent you.

When you bring the people
out of Egypt,
all of you will serve the LORD
at this very mountain."

וְהִנֵּה הַסְּנֶה בֹּעֵר בָּאֵשׁ
וְהַסְּנֶה אֵינֶנּוּ אֻכָּל

COMMENTARY

Moses was a shepherd. It seems like you have to be a shepherd before God will make you a Jewish leader. Moses works as a shepherd. Jacob works as a shepherd. Joseph was an assistant shepherd. King David was a shepherd. Maybe you have to practice leading sheep before you graduate to leading people.

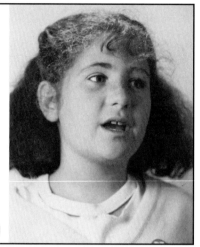

Joanna

The Jewish people are waiting as slaves in Egypt, hoping that God's promise will come true. We've had lots of stories about waiting. Abraham and Sarah, Isaac and Rebekah, Jacob and Rachel all waited to have children. Joseph waited in the pit and in the dungeon to be free. So far, God has come through on every promise.

Michael

In this story, Moses acts like a scientist. He sees something strange—a burning bush which wasn't burnt up, and and he wants to know how it works. It isn't until God talks to him, that he realizes that burning bush was a sign. Until then, it was just something interesting to investigate.

Anna

THE BURNING BUSH—A CLOSE LOOK

SECRET MESSAGES

THE PROOF IS IN THE ECHO

This story starts by telling us that God **heard, remembered, saw, and knew.** Find a place in an earlier story where God **heard.** Find a place where God **remembered.** And find a place where God **saw.** Check your answers on page 220.

QUESTIONS AND ANSWERS

In this story, MOSES asks 2 questions of God: (1) **"Who am I that I should go to Pharaoh?"** (2) **"Who am I, that I should bring out the Children of Israel?"** God then gives 2 answers: (1) **"I will be with you."** (2) "Let this be a sign for **you, for I have sent you. When you bring the people out of Egypt, all of you will serve the LORD at this very mountain."** Can you figure out how the answers fit the questions?

MAGIC WORDS

GOD OF THE FATHERS   אָנֹכִי אֱלֹהֵי אָבִיךָ

There is only one God. In this chapter, the TORAH talks about the God of ABRAHAM, the God of ISAAC, and the God of JACOB. Even though there is only one God, each of the fathers knew God in a different way. What was special about the way ABRAHAM knew God? What was special about the way ISAAC knew God? And what was special about the way JACOB knew God?

LAND OF MILK AND HONEY אֶל־אֶרֶץ זָבַת חָלָב וּדְבָשׁ

We know that a land of milk and honey is a good place, a kind of biblical candyland. We usually think that the Bible is using poetry when it talks about milk and honey, showing us that it was a sweet land. However, from studying history, we know that in those days the land of Israel was rich in goats and cows (who make **milk**) and in date palms (which produce date **honey**). It really was a land of **milk** and **honey**. If the Bible were written today, imagine what it would call Israel: A land of _____ and _____.

FROM EGYPT TO MOUNT SINAI

After talking with God at the burning bush MOSES leaves his wife and son with his father-in-law, and he goes back down to Egypt. On the way, he meets his brother AARON, who becomes his assistant. They go to Pharaoh and tell him that God has ordered him to let the Jewish people go. Pharaoh refuses. God brings 10 plagues on Egypt: Blood, Frogs, Lice, Swarms of bugs, Cattle disease, Boils, Hail, Locust, Darkness, and the Death of the firstborn. After each plague Pharaoh agrees to let the Jewish people leave, and then he changes his mind. The night before the 10th plague, MOSES orders the people to paint the blood from a lamb on their doorposts, and to make a seder. The first passover was celebrated while the Jews were still slaves in Egypt. After the death of all the firstborn sons of Egypt, Pharaoh sends the Jewish people out.

They head towards the Sea of Reeds. Pharaoh and his chariots chase them. God divides the Sea of Reeds and the children of Israel cross safely, but the Egyptian army is drowned when the waters return. Then, the Children of Israel make a series of camps as they move through the wilderness. Finally they come to Mt. Sinai.

CHAPTER 27

THE TEN COMMANDMENTS

Three months after the Children of Israel exited Egypt
they came to the wilderness of Sinai.
Israel camped before that mountain.

MOSES climbed up to God
and the LORD called to him from the mountain:
"Say this to the house of Jacob
and tell this the Children of Israel.

You have seen what I did to the Egyptians,
and how I carried you on eagles' wings
and brought you to Me.
NOW, if you will **listen** to my voice
and **keep** my commandments
and be my treasure from among all peoples,
then you shall be to Me a kingdom of priests and a holy nation."

MOSES came and called for the elders of the people.
He set before them all the **words**
which the LORD had commanded him.
The whole people answered together:
"All the LORD **said**—we will do."

MOSES returned all the people's **words** to the LORD.

The LORD said to MOSES:
"HERE—I am coming to you in a thick cloud
so that everyone can hear when I **speak** to you,
and so that they may believe you forever."

MOSES brought the people from the camp to meet God.
They stood at the bottom of the mountain.

Mount Sinai was all smoke
because the LORD came down in fire.
The smoke rose like the smoke of a furnace.
The whole mountain shook.

The LORD **said** all these **things**:

אָנֹכִי יהוה אֱלֹהֶיךָ

"I am the LORD your God,
who brought you out of the
land of Egypt, out of slavery.

לֹא תִרְצָח

Do NOT murder.

לֹא־יִהְיֶה לְךָ אֱלֹהִים

You will NOT have any other
Gods before ME. You will NOT
make any idols. Do NOT bow
down to idols or serve them.

לֹא תִנְאָף

Do NOT commit adultery.

לֹא תִשָּׂא אֶת־שֵׁם־
יהוה אֱלֹהֶיךָ לַשָּׁוְא

Do NOT use the name of
the LORD your God when
making a false promise.

לֹא תִגְנֹב

Do NOT steal.

זָכוֹר אֶת־יוֹם הַשַּׁבָּת לְקַדְּשׁוֹ

REMEMBER the Shabbat. Make
it holy. You may labor for six
days and do all your work.
But the 7th day is Shabbat.

לֹא תַעֲנֶה בְרֵעֲךָ עֵד שָׁקֶר

Do NOT lie about your
neighbor in an oath.

כַּבֵּד אֶת־אָבִיךָ וְאֶת־אִמֶּךָ

HONOR your father and
your mother.

לֹא תַחְמֹד

Do NOT wish to take over
your neighbor's house or
anything that belongs to
your neighbor."

COMMENTARY

I would have really liked to have been with the Jewish people at Mt. Sinai. It sounds like God did really fantastic special effects—it must have been exciting. Also, I think it would be great to have God teach us on the spot.

Greg

In the first chapter in this book, we started looking at tens, when God said ten things and created the world. We keep looking at tens. Ten generations, ten more generations, ten family histories and so on. I don't think ten was a magic number. I just think that it was easy to count on your fingers.

Rochelle

People always talk about the 10 commandments. They are supposed to be the most important ten things in a religion. I agree with all the commandments, but they are not the things I would pick as most important. I would have included helping those in need, not making war, and a couple of others.

Brent

THE TEN COMMANDMENTS—A CLOSE LOOK

SECRET MESSAGES

HEBREW AND ENGLISH

In HEBREW, we call them **aseret ha dibrot**, עֲשֶׂרֶת הַדִּבְּרוֹת the 10 statements. In English, we call them commandments. The problem is the first of the ten. Look at it:

> I am the LORD your God, who brought you out of the land of Egypt, out of slavery.

Can you figure out what this "statement" commands? Check your answer on page 220.

THE PATTERN

The 10 commandments were carved on two tablets, 5 commandments on each tablet. There is a pattern to the commandments. The first 5 commandments are between God and people. The next 5 commandments are for the way people should live together. This is the fifth commandment: **HONOR your father and mother**. Can you figure out why this is considered a commandment between God and people? Check your answer on page 220.

For every one of the first 5 commandments there is a matching commandment in the second 5. Use the chart below to fill in the matches.

BETWEEN GOD AND PEOPLE	BETWEEN PEOPLE	REASON
"I am the LORD. your God, who brought you out of the land of Egypt, out of slavery.		People are created in God's image. Murdering a person is like destroying God's image.
You will NOT have any other Gods before ME. You will NOT make any idols. Do NOT bow down to idols or serve them.		Adultery is when you have a pact to have a special partnership and you cheat.

Do NOT use the name of the LORD your God when making a false promise.		God's name stands for a set of rules that we live by. When you lie and swear by God that what you say is true, you are stealing in God's name.
REMEMBER the Shabbat. Make it holy. You may labor for six days and do all your work. But the 7th day is Shabbat.		The Torah says that the Shabbat is a witness to the fact that God created the world and took the Jews out of Egypt. When you don't keep Shabbat, you are being a poor witness of God's miracles.
HONOR your father and your mother.		When you wish to take over something belonging to your neighbor, you are saying that your house isn't good enough. This is not honoring your parents.

39 MORE YEARS

After the 10 commandments are heard from Mount Sinai, MOSES goes back up the mountain and spends 40 days and 40 nights getting the commandments from God. When MOSES returns, he finds the people are building a golden calf. He smashes the two tablets and has the idol burnt. MOSES then goes back up the mountain and spends another 40 days and 40 nights carving a new set of tablets. These he brings back to the people.

From there, the children of Israel spend 39 more years wandering in the wilderness. At times, the people rebel. At times they are forced to make war to defend themselves. Throughout the years, the Jewish people worship in a tent called the Tabernacle. Throughout the years, MOSES teaches Torah to the people.

At the end of the Torah, almost everyone who left Egypt with MOSES has died. A new generation is waiting to enter the land of Israel. JOSHUA is going to be the new leader of the Jewish people. He will take the people across the Jordan river and into the Promised Land. God tells MOSES that he cannot cross into Israel. The last chapter of the Torah tells the story of MOSES' death.

CHAPTER 28

ALMOST THE PROMISED LAND Deuteronomy 34:1-2

MOSES went up from the plains of Moab to Mount Nebo,
top of the Pisgah (which is across from Jericho).

The LORD showed him all the **land** of Israel.
From Gilead to Dan, all of Naphtali,
the **land** of Ephraim and Manasseh.
From all the **land** of Judah to the Mediterranean Sea.
The Negev. From the Plain of Jericho to Zoar.

The LORD said to him: "This is the **land** which I promised
to ABRAHAM, to ISAAC, and to JACOB,
saying: 'To your future-family I will give it.'

I let you see it with your own eyes.
But you will not cross into it."

MOSES, The LORD's servant, died there,
in the **land** of Moab,
By the LORD's word.

The LORD buried him in the valley of the **Land** of Moab,
and no person knows his grave to this day.

MOSES was 120 years old when he died.
His eyes were still bright
and he was still strong.

The Children of Israel wept for MOSES for 30 days.
The days of weeping for MOSES ended.

JOSHUA, son of NUN, was filled with the **spirit** of wisdom
because MOSES had touched him.
The Children of Israel listened to him.

Never again will Israel have a prophet like MOSES,
who knew the LORD face to face.

Who did all the signs and wonders
which God sent him to do in the **land** of Egypt.
To Pharaoh
and all his workers
and all his **land**.

And all the mighty hand
and all the wonders
which MOSES made happen
before the eyes of all Israel.

וְלֹא קָם נָבִיא עוֹד בְּיִשְׂרָאֵל כְּמֹשֶׁה

COMMENTARY

I feel sad for Moses. He spends his whole life leading the Jewish people home, and then he can't go with them. I guess he is kind of like a parent who has to let his children grow up and go on their own. I bet he was both crying and smiling when he looked across into the land of Israel.

Andrea

You know, it takes almost the whole Torah for God's promises to Abraham to come true. At the end of the Torah, the children of Israel are finally a great people, and now they are finally getting the land God promised to Abraham's future-family.

Danny

The first people in the Torah were Adam and Eve. God brings them clothes. The last person in the Torah is Moses. God is kind to him and buries him. In the Torah, God not only gives rules for people to live by, but God also sets a good example by doing the right thing.

Kenny

ALMOST THE PROMISED LAND—A CLOSE LOOK

REPEATED WORDS

MAGIC NUMBER

In this story, the word **land** is repeated. What do you think the Torah wanted to teach us by making this word stand out? Check your answer on page 220.

WORD ECHOES

In this chapter God tells MOSES that a promise was made to ABRAHAM, a promise was made to ISAAC, and a promise was made to JACOB that their future-family would inherit the land of ISRAEL. Find each of those promises.

MAGIC WORDS

AND NO PERSON KNOWS HIS GRAVE וְלֹא־יָדַע אִישׁ אֶת־קְבֻרָתוֹ

When a famous person dies, we usually make his or her tomb a place for people to visit and remember that person. Why do you think that God buried MOSES in a secret place?

וְלֹא־קָם נָבִיא עוֹד בְּיִשְׂרָאֵל כְּמֹשֶׁה

NEVER AGAIN WILL ISRAEL HAVE A PROPHET LIKE MOSES

Make a list of things that made MOSES a great leader. Decide which of those things was special to MOSES.

A rabbi once told his students that he had a dream about facing God after he died. The rabbi said that God judged him and asked him the one question he most feared. The students asked: "Were you afraid that God would ask you why you weren't as great a leader as MOSES?" The rabbi said: "No, I am not MOSES." "Were you afraid that God would ask you why you weren't as great a teacher as MOSES?" The rabbi said: "No, I am not MOSES." "Then what was the question?" the students asked. The rabbi said: "I am afraid that God will ask me why I haven't been the best possible me I could have been." What are some ways you could come closer to the best possible you?

BEGINNINGS

BOOKENDS

Created is the word at the beginning and the end of this story. This story is all about creation. The word created is used only one other time in this story. For every other step in creation, the Torah uses the word made. The only other time the word created is used, is when God made people. Why do you think the Torah wanted this one step of creation to be different?

CLUE ONE: Make a list of things you have made. Then make a second list of things you have created.

CLUE TWO: Look at the 6 times when God says "GOOD" and the 1 time where God says "VERY GOOD."

MAGIC NUMBERS

In this story, you find the words *God said 10 times. God created the world through ten sayings. What other "ten" does this remind you of?

Why do you think the Torah wants us to find a connection between the ten sayings of creation and the ten_____?

EATING THE FRUIT

FIND THE DIFFERENCE

God said about the TREE THE OF KNOWLEDGE OF GOOD FROM EVIL: "You are not to eat from it." EVE told the snake that God said: "You cannot eat it, and you cannot touch it." EVE added "You cannot touch it" on her own.

THE GARDEN

HIDDEN X-PATTERNS

In the beginning of the story we meet two special trees, the TREE OF LIFE and the TREE THE OF KNOWLEDGE OF GOOD FROM EVIL. We are told that these trees are in the middle of the garden. At the end of the story, when people have eaten from the tree, they wind up hiding in the middle of the trees of the garden. When people do wrong, everything gets turned around.

At the beginning of the story, the LORD makes ADAM out of the dust of the soil. At the end of the story, ADAM and EVE are told that they must work the soil to earn their food, and that their bodies will return to dust after they die. One idea which comes from this story is the idea that life is a circle. Peoples' lives begin with the earth. We grow food in the earth. And in the end we will be buried in the earth.

X-patterns are one way the Torah gets us to look closely at certain words.

CAIN AND ABEL

MAGIC SEVENS

Seven is the key to this story. ABEL's name is used 7 times and CAIN's name is used 14 (7+7) times. We know from the story that CAIN was not twice as important as ABEL. Something else is going on. The most important word in this story is brothers. It is also used 7 times. Seven connects CAIN and ABEL as brothers. Brothers and sisters should be the people who help each other the most. That isn't always the case. Brothers and sisters also know how to hurt each other (and sometimes do).

AN X-PATTERN

This x-pattern is made up of the words bloods and soil. In the story of the GARDEN we learned that the word ADAM, which means people, includes the word DAM which means blood. We also learned that the word AHDAMAH, which means ground includes both DAM (blood) AND ADAM (people). People are made up of blood, and people have a partnership with the soil. This story teaches us that when people fight and spill blood, they destroy their special partnership with the soil.

AND INTRODUCING NOAH

MAGIC NUMBERS

NOAH was the 10th generation. Remember that number, it will help us later.

LIKE PARENT LIKE CHILD

People were created in God's image. When people do what is right, they come out like God. Here, when people's **hearts** thought only evil, God's **heart** was pained because people weren't living up to God's image.

FIND THE CHANGE

LAMECH blamed God for cursing the soil when it was really ADAM and EVE who cursed the soil by their actions. Since leaving the Garden of Eden, people's partnership with the soil hasn't been working right. CAIN also made it worse. (Look at the story of CAIN and ABEL and see if you can find how he had the soil cursed).

A CONNECTION

A name can be an important thing. LAMECH named NOAH comfort, hoping that God would become **comfortable** once again with people. God was **uncomfortable** with people because of the ways they were acting. God, however, did find one person whose actions are **comfortable** (and right). That one righteous person was NOAH.

NOAH

MAGIC NUMBERS

The Torah uses the word **covenant** seven times. A covenant is a bargain or a contract between two sides. Here God and people make a covenant. God promises never to destroy the world again and gives people some rules to follow. There was no covenant between God and ADAM and EVE, so this covenant between God and NOAH is the first one. It is so **important** that the word **covenant** is used 7 times.

FIND THE DIFFERENCE

When God blessed ADAM and EVE, God told them to master the world. This time, God set up a covenant to help people master the world in the right way.

HARD STUFF

This whole story is build like a pyramid. every one of the first six parts has a matching part in the second half of the story. It looks like this:

If you look closely at the words in each part, you will find that usually one set of words in each part of the first half is repeated in the matching part in the second half. Sometimes the matching parts use opposite words. In the first half of the story God floods everything that had been created (except for NOAH and his family). In the second half of the story God takes away the flood and rebuilds creation with NOAH's family. God gives them a covenant as a way of guiding how people should live. The pattern of this story shows how the covenant is the center of this second creation.

THE TOWER OF BABEL

SECRET PLANS

Just like the NOAH story, this story has two halves. In the first half of the story, people move to the Valley of Shinar and decide to build a Tower to the sky. They do it in order to **make a name** and to keep themselves from being **scattered over the face of the earth**. In the second half the story, God sees the tower and decides that it is not good. God confuses everyone by babbling languages. In the end, no one has a famous **name** because no one understands anyone else, and people are **scattered over the face of the earth**.

The story is built out of an X-pattern. In the beginning, **aLL the earth** was one **language**. In the end, God babbled the **language** of **all the earth**.

AND INTRODUCING ABRAM

MAGIC NUMBERS

There were **10 sayings** before the story of ADAM and EVE. There were 10 generations from ADAM to NOAH. Now there are 10 generations from NOAH to ABRAM. ADAM and EVE were one beginning. NOAH was another beginning. Now ABRAM, who is the first Jew, is another beginning.

MYSTERY

The Bible doesn't tell us anything about ABRAM or SARAI as children. The first Bible story about them starts with them as adults. While there are famous stories about ABRAM smashing the idols and discovering God on his own, these stories aren't in the Bible. They are found in another collection of stories called the MIDRASH.

ABRAM: LEAVING HOME

MAGIC NUMBERS

ABRAM's name is used **7** times. The **land** is used **7** times too. Matching the two, we learn that ABRAM and his family belong in the **land** of Israel. That is the promise God makes as soon as they come to Canaan. But there is more. God gives **7** blessings to ABRAM. It is almost a mathematical formula.

ABRAM=Blessing=The **land**.

A SECRET CONNECTION

God tells ABRAM: "Take yoursel from your land . . . to the land: there I will let you see." Some people think that this sentence means that God wouldn't tell ABRAM where he was going until he arrives. Other people think that this sentence means that God would appear to ABRAM once he came to the land of Canaan. Once ABRAM comes to Canaan, the Torah tells us: **The LORD was seen by ABRAM**. It could be that ABRAM went to a strange land in order to know God better. This is not the only possible answer.

ABRAM: LOT LEAVES

FIND THE CHANGE

When ABRAM's family first came to Canaan, the "wealth" belonged to the whole family. The Torah says: **ABRAM took SARAI his wife, and LOT his brother's son, and all they owned.** When they came back from Egypt, ABRAM and LOT had already divided the wealth into two separate fortunes. The Torah says: **ABRAM went up from Egypt. He and his wife, and all that was his.**

The big feud in this story is over belongings. The Torah tells us: **They had so many belongings that they were not able to SETTLE together.**

REPEATED WORDS

Sometimes the TORAH doesn't use a word 5, 7, 10, or 12 times in order to make it stand out. Sometimes a word stands out just because it is used often. In this story SETTLE is used 6 times and **land** is used 8 times. These aren't "magic numbers," but both words are important. In this story we see the Jewish people **settling** in the **land** of Canaan.

A TWO PART PROMISE

At this point, the Jewish people are only ABRAM and SARAI. They have no children, they have left their homeland, and are just camping all over the land of Canaan. God makes two promises: (1) To give them a large family, and (2) to give the land of Canaan to that family. At this point, nothing has come true and ABRAM is asked to hang onto promises.

Back in chapter 7, LEAVING HOME: God tells ABRAM: **"And I will make you a great nation** and **To your future-family I will give this land."** Here the same two promises are repeated.

ABRAM: A COVENANT

REPEATED WORDS

In this story, the words **future-family** and **inherit** are each repeated. These two words stand for the two promises God made to ABRAM. Your **future-family** will be so many that you can't count them. Your children will **inherit** the land of Israel.

TWO-PART PROMISE

The first promise was: **"I will make you a great nation."** ABRAM asks God: **"My Master the LORD what could You give me? I have no children."** He is really asking: "How can I be a great nation if my wife and I can't even give birth to one son?" The second promise was: **"All the land which you see, I give it to you and to your future-family forever."** ABRAM asks God: **"How do I know that I will inherit it?"** ABRAM is really asking: "Since I don't own it now, how do I know that my future-family will inherit it later?"

WORD ECHOES

In chapter 1, BEGINNINGS, we find that God made the stars to be **signs** and **placed them in the sky to give light on the earth.** In the story of THE GARDEN, we learn **The LORD God formed the HUMAN from the dust of the soil.** In chapter 8, LOT LEAVES, God promises ABRAM that his future-family will be as many as the **dust of the land.**

Both the number of stars and the number of grains of soil are infinite. There are more of them than you can count. With these two word echoes God promises ABRAM a very large family. But there is an echo of something else, too. By being like **the dust of the earth,** his family is like the first HUMAN—ADAM—connected to all people. By being like stars, his family becomes a sign and source of light.

ABRAM BECOME ABRAHAM

MAGIC NUMBER

In this story ABRAM's new name, **ABRAHAM,** is used 10 times. This is just like the 10 sayings in creation, the 10 generations before NOAH, and the 10 generations between NOAH and ABRAM. Sometimes something used 10 times gives us a clue to a new beginning. Here, ABRAHAM's new name, along with the covenant and the mitzvah of circumcision, forms a new beginning for ABRAHAM.

FIND THE CONNECTION

The Torah introduces NOAH using 3 words. **NOAH was a righteous person. He was the best in his generation. NOAH walked with God.** Here the Torah used the same three words: **righteous,** the **best,** and **walking** before or with God, about ABRAM. Both men were new beginnings for the world. NOAH begins the new world after the flood, and ABRAM will begin the Jewish people and their special partnership with God.

KEEP THE COVENANT

In chapter 2, THE GARDEN, God places humans in the Garden **to work and keep it.** In chapter 3, CAIN AND ABEL, CAIN asks: **"Am I my brother's keeper."** God's answer is yes. In this story God tells ABRAHAM to **keep** the covenant. God wants people to be keepers. The Hebrew word for **keeper** is **shomer.** It means a guard or a watcher.

SARAH LAUGHED

ACTION VERBS

In this story,
Please is used 3 times,
Hurry is used 3 times
and ABRAHAM **runs** 2 times (rather than walking).

You get the feeling that ABRAHAM is trying as hard as possible to make the guests feel welcome. ABRAHAM is hurrying as fast as he can to serve his guests from the best of what he has.

In this story, ABRAHAM is a model for teaching us that making visitors and strangers welcome is a mitzvah.

FIND WHAT CHANGED

When SARAH laughed at the idea of having a son, she said that both she and ABRAHAM were too old. When God reported SARAH's thoughts to ABRAHAM, God only told him the part about SARAH being too old. God didn't tell him that SARAH also thought that ABRAHAM was too old. Perhaps God cared about ABRAHAM and didn't want to hurt his feelings.

THE SODOM DEBATE

MAGIC SEVEN

The word **righteous** is used seven times in this story. This story is all about being **righteous**. ABRAHAM shows us that a **tzadik** has to more than just avoid the wrong. The **tzadik** must also stand up for what is right.

ISAAC IS BORN

THE CONNECTOR

In the story FROM ABRAM TO ABRAHAM, God promises ABRAHAM that SARAH will have a son, and ABRAHAM laughs. God tells him to name his son ISAAC (meaning he laughs). In the story SARAH LAUGHS, first the messengers and then God tell ABRAHAM that ABRAHAM will have a son. SARAH hears this and laughs. Both ABRAHAM and SARAH are too old to have children, but God makes a promise. One thing this story teaches us is that it takes a mother, a father, and God to make a child. All three are partners.

THE BINDING OF ISAAC ANSWERS

A CONNECTING ECHO

This order God gives ABRAHAM has some echoes of the way God called him for the first time. In chapter 7, LEAVING HOME, God says: **"Take yourself from your land, from your birthplace from your father's house to the land: there I will let you see."** In both places, God gives an order with three phrases that describe the hard part of the test that follows. In both places, God tells ABRAHAM that the final **seeing** or **hearing** will happen once ABRAHAM goes to the testing place.

The story of ABRAHAM is made up of ten tests. The first test was when God asked him to LEAVE HIS HOME. The BINDING OF ISAAC was the last test. See if you remember all ten of these tests: (1) leaving Haran, (2) going to Egypt, (3) separating from LOT, (4) rescuing LOT, (5) having ISHMAEL born, (6) being circumcised, (7) arguing for Sodom, (8) going to ABIMELECH, (9) sending ISHMAEL away, and (10) the binding of ISAAC.

MAGIC NUMBERS

In this story, the word son is used **10** times. This story is about the future of ABRAHAM's **son**. His son's future is the future of the Jewish people.

The word **see** is an important word in the ABRAHAM story. His adventure began when God told him to **"go to the land—there I will let you see."** When ABRAHAM reaches that land he sees God. Now ABRAHAM goes to a mountain whose name, **MORIAH**, means **see**ing, and he names the place **ADONAI-YIREH** (meaning the LORD sees). The Hebrew word for prophet is NAVI, which **means** one who sees.

REBEKAH AT THE WELL

THE HIDDEN TEST

The servant's test was to find a woman ready to do the right thing. He hoped that when he asked for water for himself—**"Please—may I drink from your jar?"**—the right woman would know that the camels needed water, too. The woman had to do CHESED, more than what was asked.

FIND THE CHANGE

When we compare what the servant wanted the right woman to say with what REBEKAH actually said, we can see two changes.

The servant wanted her to say: **"Drink,"** and REBEKAH said: **"Drink, my master."** She added her own words of respect.

The servant wanted her to say: **"I will also draw water for your camels."** She did, but she added something: **"I will also draw water for your camels—until they have finished drinking."**

She showed even more CHESED than the servant wanted.

SECRET WORD CONNECTIONS

In this story, REBEKAH welcomes strangers like ABRAHAM did. She **hurries** and **runs** to bring water. ABRAHAM **hurries and runs** to bring food and drink to the strangers in the story SARAH LAUGHS.

REBEKAH MEETS ISAAC

A CONNECTION

LABAN and BETHUEL's blessing was: **May you become a thousand times many and may your future-family inherit the cities of their enemies.** When God blessed ABRAHAM at the end of THE BINDING OF ISAAC, this was part of the blessing. **I will make you many . . . many . . . Your future-family shall inherit the cities of their enemies.** These two blessings have the same two parts. Both blessings talk about the same two things God has always promised ABRAHAM: (1) you will be father of a great nation, and (2) your future-family will inherit the land of Israel. ISAAC will inherit ABRAHAM's blessing, and so it seems that he and REBEKAH will have the same future.

LOVE AT FIRST SIGHT

In this story, ISAAC **lifted up his eyes and saw** . . . . REBEKAH **lifted up her eyes and saw** . . . The next instant they are in love and then married.

COMFORT

In the story of the GARDEN, the Torah says: **(This is why a man leaves his father and mother and clings to his wife and they become one).** This is exactly what happens to ISAAC—with his mother dead, he now clings to REBEKAH.

JACOB: ROUND 1 AND 2

MAGIC NUMBERS

These magic numbers help us see that both of ISAAC's sons are important. Both will be fathers of nations. This is just like God blessing both ISAAC and ISHMAEL. Even though only one son will lead the Jewish people, both are blessed because they are part of ABRAHAM's future-family.

CONNECTION

Both SARAH and REBEKAH have trouble becoming pregnant. Both times, God listens to their husbands' prayers. Both times, God makes predictions about their sons. God was a partner in the birth of ISAAC and in the birth of the twins.

JACOB: ROUND 3

2 MATCHING CLUE

In this story, the Torah says:

> REBEKAH heard what ISAAC said to **ESAU his son**.
> ESAU went out to the field to hunt game,
> and REBEKAH said to **JACOB her son**.

Here we see that each parent is still playing favorites. Even though ISAAC is father to both sons, and even though REBEKAH is mother to both sons, each thought of one of the boys as being "my son."

FIND THE MISSING PART

In repeating the blessing to ESAU, ISAAC tells him about all the new blessings which he gave to JACOB. These are all blessings that have to do with the **land** being good to JACOB. What ISAAC left out were the many blessings God gave to ABRAHAM and that were passed on from father to son.

> May nations serve you,
> and may peoples bow to you . . . .
> Let those who curse you be cursed.
> Let those who **bless** you be **blessed**."

JACOB'S DREAM

MAGIC NUMBERS

In this story, the word God is used 10 times. This story is all about the new partnership between God and JACOB. God tells JACOB 10 things. The first of these things even sounds like the first of the 10 commandments—**I am the LORD your God**. At the end of the story, JACOB promises to tithe everything he owns for God. A tithe is taking 10 percent of everything you have and setting it aside for God's work.

FIND THE CONNECTION

God gives a blessing very much like this to ABRAM in chapter 8, LOT LEAVES. That was the blessing that God gave him after he split his family. It was the first full blessing given to ABRAM in the land of Israel. Here, God's blessing to JACOB is the first blessing given to him. It happens right after he leaves his family and just before he leaves the land of Israel.

DOUBLE WEDDINGS

MAGIC NUMBERS

The 10 times RACHEL's name is used is just like the 10 times that JACOB's name is used in chapter 17, ROUNDS 1 AND 2, and the 10 times that BLESS is used during JACOB's blessing. The Torah is making a connection. RACHEL will become the next important mother of the Jewish people.

The word avad, **serve** is used 7 times. This word also means **slaving**. JACOB is tricked by LABAN. He is almost a slave. This story reminds us of what will happen when the Jews come to Egypt. The Haggadah says: **A wandering Aramean tried to destroy our father**. It explains that LABAN is the wandering Aramean who made a slave out of JACOB. We learn that slavery can destroy us.

FIND THE CONNECTION

LABAN gave ZILPAH to LEAH as a servant and gave BILHAH to RACHEL as a servant. In the next story, both BILHAH and ZILPAH also become secondary-wives to JACOB, giving birth to some of JACOB's 12 sons.

ROUND 4: WRESTLING

MAGIC NUMBERS

The stories in this chapter are all about **crossing**. When you **cross**, you leave one side behind and come to something new. In this chapter, JACOB leaves LABAN behind and returns to the land God gave his family. He meets his brother ESAU and leaves behind all the anger from their childhood struggle. He goes through a night of struggle and leaves the JACOB (heel grabbing) part of his life behind and becomes ISRAEL (the one who wrestles with God). Then JACOB leaves ESAU and goes his own way seeking God. In the 12 times JACOB **crosses** in this story, he grows into a new person—ISRAEL.

These stories are also built around the word **face**. When JACOB is getting ready to meet his brother ESAU, the word face is used 4 times. JACOB says: **I will wipe the anger from his face**. Thinking about his brother, he sees his face. When he spends the night wrestling, he is given a new name and says: **I have seen God face to face**. This is the night that changed JACOB into Israel, and face is used 4 times. When he finally meets ESAU, JACOB says: **When I look in your face, it is like seeing the face of God**. For JACOB, making peace with his brother is like the blessing he received after the night of struggling. It was like seeing God's face. His fear of his brother's face becomes a chance to see God's image.

THE CONNECTING "HAND, NAME, and BLESSING"

Many of the things in this story bring us back to chapter 17, ROUNDS 1 AND 2 where JACOB steals ESAU's first-born right and blessing. As he thinks about meeting his brother, we and JACOB are both reminded of the last time the brothers were together. In order to steal the blessing, REBEKAH covers JACOB's hands so they are like ESAU's hands. When ISAAC is getting ready to bless him, ISAAC says: **The voice is the voice of JACOB but the hands are the hands of ESAU**. In this story, as JACOB thinks about meeting ESAU, the word **hand** comes up over and over. It is as if he remembers that day, and all he can think about is his hands pretending to be ESAU's hands.

The same thing happens with his name and the blessing. When ESAU learns that JACOB stole the blessing, he shouts: **That is why he is named JACOB** (meaning the one who grabs heels)—**he has grabbed from me two times**. In this story, JACOB asks for a new blessing, one he doesn't steal, and gets a new name that isn't connected to stealing. JACOB has struggled with God and people and learned how to make peace. He has changed and become ISRAEL. This is his real blessing.

BIRTHS AND DEATHS

FIND THE CHANGE

The biggest difference between these two name changes is that the first one came from a "man" (who might be an angel) and the second one came from God. The first time, the man explains the reason for the name ISRAEL as coming from the struggling that JACOB did with God. This time, God doesn't explain—the Torah just says: "God called him ISRAEL." JACOB earned this name.

AN ECHO

Be fruitful and become many is the blessing God gave to the first life that was created, and to NOAH and his family. Each time this blessing marked a beginning. Now JACOB and his family have become a nation. They are living in the land God promised them. This is a new beginning.

A PROMISE COMES TRUE

While God has given lots of blessings, there were two major parts to the covenant: (1) God promised to make ABRAHAM's family into a nation and (2) God promised to give them the land of Israel.

God also promised:

> And I will make you a great nation,
> And I will BLESS you.
> And I will make your name great.
> And you will be a BLESSING.
> And I will BLESS those who BLESS you
> (And I will curse anyone who curses you).
> All the families of the earth will be BLESSED.

God predicted:

> Your **future-family** will be strangers
> in a land which is not theirs.
> They shall be slaves and suffer for 400 years.
> But I will punish the nation they serve,
> and after that, they will exit with riches.

God also promised JACOB:

> I am with you.
> **I will keep you** in all your goings
> **and I will return** you to this soil
> because **I will not leave you**
> until **I have done all that I promised** you.

So far, ABRAHAM has become the father of many nations. The Jewish people have grown and become rich. Many of the promises have come true.

THE DREAMS COME TRUE

A MAGIC NUMBER

This is the family history of JACOB is the tenth family history in the Torah. Remember, NOAH was the tenth generation after ADAM, and ABRAHAM was the tenth generation after NOAH. Each of them brought a new beginning. JACOB's family also brings a new beginning. With JACOB's family, the Jewish people become a nation.

Usually, a family history lists all the children who are becoming the future-family. In this family history, we hear only about JOSEPH. We don't hear anything about his 11 brothers. What is important to the Torah is what happens to JOSEPH, because that shapes the new beginning of this family history.

AN ECHO

JOSEPH's two dreams remind us of the pictures God gave ABRAHAM. God said that the Jewish people would be as many as the stars of the sky. JOSEPH has a dream about the stars. God told ABRAHAM that the Jewish people would cover the land the way the sands do. JOSEPH has a dream that takes place on the land. JACOB and JOSEPH's brothers think his dreams are selfish, but we should remember that they are dreams about the future of the Jewish people.

THE DREAMS COME TRUE PART 2

REPEATED WORDS

When the brothers think about killing JOSEPH, REUBEN says: **Spill no blood.** These words echo God's words to CAIN: **From now on, you are cursed from the soil because the soil opened up its mouth to take your brother's bloods from your hand.** It also echos one of the commandments God gave to NOAH: **And also for your blood, I will seek responsibility from every person for the life of her brother or sister . . . because God created people in God's image.** The Torah reminds us to be a "keeper."

218

THE DREAMS COME TRUE PART 4

GOOD THINGS HAPPEN TWICE

In the dungeon, JOSEPH (2) **succeeds**, (3) **finds favor**, and is (4) **is put in charge** of the dungeon because (1) **the LORD was with him**. When something happens only once, we may think it is just an accident. When it happens twice, there has to be a reason. When he succeeds a second time in the dungeon, we know for sure that it is because **the LORD was with him**.

THE HAND IS QUICKER THAN THE EYE

JOSEPH **finds favor in** both POTIPHAR's **eyes** and in the dungeon-master's **eyes**. Potiphar's wife only **sets her eyes** upon him. POTIPHAR and the dungeon-master see that JOSEPH will succeed. They know the LORD is with JOSEPH. Potiphar's wife only sees JOSEPH from the outside. She wants to be with him for the wrong reasons.

People **work** with their hands and hold things they **own** in their hands. In telling the JOSEPH story, the Torah often uses the word **hand**. In this part of the story JOSEPH goes from the **hand** of the Ishmaelites and becomes POTIPHAR's slave. Then, because everything succeeds in his **hands**, POTIPHAR **leaves** everything he owns in JOSEPH's **hands**. JOSEPH goes from slave to manager. When JOSEPH runs away from Potiphar's wife, he **leaves** his coat in her **hands**. It was good for JOSEPH when POTIPHAR **left** everything in his **hands**. JOSEPH is thrown in the dungeon when he **leaves** his coat in the wife's **hands**. In a way, this story show us how people can do either good or bad with their hands.

The Torah describes RACHEL as being **nicely shaped and nice to look at**. JOSEPH is RACHEL's son. She was JACOB's favorite wife, he was JACOB's favorite son. RACHEL remained a good sister to LEAH even after she became JACOB's first wife. If JOSEPH was like his mother, what do you think he will be like in the stories to come?

THE DREAMS COME TRUE PART 7

THE RULE ABOUT TWO DREAMS

JOSEPH tells PHARAOH: PHARAOH had two dreams because **this thing is true. It came from God and God will quickly do it**. If having two dreams with the same meaning tells us that something is true, then we know that JOSEPH's dreams about his brothers bowing down must come true.

REPEATED SENTENCE

PHARAOH uses the same words the butcher and the baker used: "**I have dreamed a dream and there is no one to tell what it means.**" But JOSEPH was there in jail when PHARAOH needed him. Both times JOSEPH says, "**true meanings must come from God.**" Once again, this second time shows us that this is true.

HAND, EYES, and CLOTHES

This time, JOSEPH finds favor in PHARAOH's **eyes**, and the signet ring is placed on his **hands**. Once more he is put in charge. Finally, he has a new **robe** which means a new beginning. Now we know for sure that **God has been with him**, and that all the dreams will come true. JOSEPH is like a king, and can use his power to save human life.

A NEW KING

MAGIC NUMBERS

The Torah lists 5 different ways the Children of Israel grew: (1) The children of Israel were **fruitful**. (2) They **increased**. (3) They **became many**. (4) They **became very very strong**. (5) They **filled the land**. Then the Torah lists 5 different things that Pharaoh did: (1) **He put taskmasters to make them suffer** while they worked. (2) The Egyptians **made SLAVES of the Children of Israel**. (3) **They made their life bitter**. (4) The King of Egypt spoke to the **Hebrew's midwives**. And when that didn't work, (5) **Pharaoh commanded his whole people**: "Every Hebrew son which is born you will throw into the river." The five words for growth and the five things Pharaoh did to hurt the Jewish people show how this sentence is true: **The more they made them suffer, the more they multiplied.**

The word **midwife** is used 7 times to make sure we notice how important these women were. We usually think of a hero as being a prince or a soldier or a famous person. These two Egyptian women were ordinary people who simply refused to do what was wrong. This makes them very important models for us.

The Children of Israel are now slaves in the land of Egypt. They are waiting for the promise to come true and for God to take them out.

AND INTRODUCING MOSES

REPEATED WORDS

This chapter tells the story of how 3 "daughters" all save and help MOSES. First, MOSES's mother, a **daughter** of the tribe of Levi, risks her life to hide her son. She shows us courage. Second, Pharaoh's **daughter** breaks her father's command, and adopts MOSES. She does CHESED—what is right. Finally, MOSES marries ZIPPORAH, JETHRO's **daughter**. She stands by MOSES. These three woman helped MOSES grow into the leader he will become.

ECHOES

After the flood NOAH was the one to rebuild the world. When NOAH rode in the ark, the future of the world rode with him. After the flood, God gave him commandments and a covenant. Now MOSES is riding in an **ark**. Later, he will save the Jewish people. Still later, God will teach MOSES the commandments and give him the covenant for the Jewish people. MOSES and NOAH were alike.

In the story Beginnings, God looks at everything as it is created. God sees that it is **good**. In this story, MOSES' mother looks at him and sees that he is **good**. Every baby is a new creation, but hearing this word GOOD makes us think that MOSES will bring a new beginning.

THE BURNING BUSH

THE PROOF IS IN THE ECHO

Everything that happened to the Jewish people in the Exodus happened before to ABRAHAM and SARAH, to IAAAC and REBEKAH, and to JACOB, RACHEL, and LEAH. Even though life in Egypt was hard, the Jewish people had proof that God would help them. If they remembered their family history, they **knew for a fact** that God would **keep** his covenant with ABRAHAM. Here are some of the examples:

God **heard** the suffering of HAGAR, the voice of ISHMAEL, the voices of LEAH and of RACHEL.

God **remembered** NOAH and those with him on the ark, as well as ABRAHAM and SARAH. God also remembered RACHEL.

God **saw** the suffering of both LEAH and JACOB.

THE TEN COMMANDMENTS

HEBREW AND ENGLISH

Jewish scholars have been arguing over the first commandment for over 2,000 years. Some people think that it is just an introduction, others think that it is a commandment to believe in one God. Some Jews think that it is possible to command people to believe in God. Some Jews don't believe that it is possible to command people to believe in one God, but they believe that it is possible to command them to do right. You will have to make your own decision about the first commandment (or statement).

THE PATTERN

The Jewish tradition teaches that **HONOR your father and mother** is a commandment between God and people because, for children, parents are like God. When parents do a good job, they are acting as God's representatives. We don't always understand our parents' orders. We don't always understand God's commandments. But we know that both God and our parents are doing the best possible thing for us. Not respecting parents is not respecting God's authority.

ALMOST THE PROMISED LAND

MAGIC NUMBERS

In this story, the word **land** is repeated. All the way back in chapter 7, LEAVING HOME, land was used 7 times. In that story God brought ABRAM to the land of Canaan to give that land to him. Since then the Jewish people have grown into a mighty nation, and they are ready to own the land, letting the laws of the Torah rule that land. It has taken the whole Torah to bring people from the Garden and get them ready to live by God's rules. Reaching the land of Israel brings the Torah to an end, but there is much more to the Jewish adventure.

BEING TORAH STARRED

Cain—Benjamin Cutter
Abel—Brett Felsher
Noah—Michael Wolfson

Abraham—David Milman
Sarah—Judi Domroy
Hagar—Stephanie Lorman
Ishamel—Randy Shaffer
Baby Isaac—Alison Fogel

Eliezer—Michael Janovici
Rebekah—Alona Thal
Laban—Grant Zeidman
Isaac—Loren Ettinger

Esau—Scott Burack
Jacob—Brent Bodner
Rachel—Sasha Gross
Leah—Roni Kurshner
Bilhah—Stephanie Lorman

Joseph—Eitan Kadosh
Potiphar's Wife—Shelly Pack

Pharaoh—Michael Jerugian
Pharaoh's Daughter—Sabrina Ingber
Yocheved—Hanna Signer
Miriam—Ophira Carr
Baby Moses—Alison Fogel
Moses—Josh Cohen

Angel—Adam Rocusin
Angel—Brett Felsher
Angel—Greg Cambell
Egyptian Guard—Jamie Wolf
Jewish Victim—Rashi Freeman-Cohen

Jacob's Brothers and
The Children of Israel
Tamir Katz
Yaariv Katz
Michael Fox
James Wolf
Seth Cohen
Greg Jaffe
Joshua Hornstein
Richard Pasque
Matt Rosenfeld
Jamie Bars
Rashi Freeman-Cohen
Jordan Applebaum

and introducing Kenny Altman as Lot.

Directed by—
Joel Lurie Grishaver

Make-Up and Catering—
Paul Glaser
A Fair With Flair

Production Crew:
Roz Silver
Steven Feinholtz
Lizabeth Fogel

Costume Design -
Golub and Rowe Design
Production Design
Image Builders Inc.
Special Effects -
Acme Judaica

Additional Costumes -
Western Costume
Props -
Universal Studios
Ellis Mercantile

Shot on Location at
Tree People Forest
and Alan's mother's bathroom

Titles—American Typesetting

Special thanks to:
Temple Emanuel, Beverly Hills
Pasedena Jewish Center
Temple Beth El, San Pedro
The New Reform Congregation, Encino
Betty Frishman
Cantor Janece Erman